John F. Kennedy:
Catholic and Humanist

John F. Kennedy:
Catholic and Humanist

Albert J. Menendez

℞ *Prometheus Books*
1203 Kensington Avenue
Buffalo, New York 14215

For Shirley

Published by Prometheus Books
1203 Kensington Avenue, Buffalo, New York 14215

Library of Congress Card Number 78-68139
ISBN 0-87975-109-6

Printed in the United States of America

Table of Contents

PREFACE

"It is now time for 'rerevision' on John Fitzgerald Kennedy. The pundits, the experts, the OpEd-page political geniuses have written him off as an unimportant president. Now another generation of more serious thinkers and writers are reanalyzing the Kennedy contribution to American life.

Albert Menendez explores with skill, insight, and sympathy the religious dimension of John F. Kennedy, and concludes that the Kennedy legacy to American life was immensely important. The American people—who still consider John Kennedy one of their greatest leaders—will certainly agree. As the first book in the 'rereappraisal' of John F. Kennedy, Mr. Menendez's volume deserves widespread interest and careful reading. I think it's an excellent book."

(Rev.) Andrew M. Greeley
Director,
Center for the Study of
American Pluralism

INTRODUCTION

Americans have a continuing fascination with the institution of the presidency and the occupants of that hallowed office. The never-ending spate of books on the presidents attests to this. We want to know everything about them—their families, recreation, favorite books, food, scandals, even their religion. The religious views of our presidents have long absorbed the time and talents of authors and journalists. With John F. Kennedy, there was a particular urgency and interest because of his Roman Catholic faith. In this book we shall try to unravel the religious complexity of this very private man.

What, then, is known about the inner John F. Kennedy? First and foremost, as family friend Cardinal Cushing remarked: "President Kennedy wore his religion, like his patriotism, lightly."[1] This is the fundamental dilemma in trying to delve beneath the surface and discover the religious side of John F. Kennedy. James Reston, in a June 1976 *New York Times* column, claimed that Kennedy was not a deeply religious man, that he did not "really believe" in his faith and thus convinced his critics that they had nothing to fear. This view echoed critiques of Kennedy's religion by otherwise sympathetic Protestants during his campaign. Episcopal Bishop James A. Pike said that Kennedy seemed to be a "thoroughgoing secularist, who really believes that a man's religion and

his decision making can be kept in two watertight compartments.''[2] Presbyterian theologian Robert McAfee Brown thought Kennedy was "a rather irregular Christian," and Lutheran historian Martin Marty saw Kennedy as "spiritually rootless."[3] Even his wife Jacqueline reportedly told Arthur Krock that he was "such a poor Catholic" that she could not understand non-Catholic fears of his becoming President.[4]

Many of those close to Kennedy ardently disagreed. His mother, Rose, in a letter challenging Reston's statement, asserted unequivocally that her son "did believe in and practiced his religion." "Although not demonstrative in his practice of religion," she continued, "or talkative about his beliefs, he attended church regularly, was a frequent communicant at Mass, and understood the meaning and value of daily prayer." She also remembered that "on the day of his inauguration, I was especially gratified to discover him at an early morning Mass, starting his Presidency by offering his mind and heart, and expressing his hopes and fears, to Almighty God, and asking His blessing as he began his great duties."[5]

Cardinal Cushing agreed with Mrs. Kennedy's assessment. "He felt his religion profoundly. It was as natural for him to be a good Catholic as it was to be a good American, and neither loyalty encumbered his buoyant spirit. After he entered the White House, President Kennedy became even more conscious than formerly of the way in which the fortunes of men and nations stand under the Providence of God ... I was close to John Kennedy at those moments of his life which were most meaningful—his marriage, the family christenings, the death of his infant children. I can testify that he was a man of strong religious commitments."[6]

Cushing also mentions that Kennedy's father had told him that the President never "failed to spend some moments on his knees in prayer" before retiring.[7]

This fundamental duality of opinion challenged me as I began this book. Who was right? Can we ever know for sure? Will it even be possible to discover credible evidence upon which to render an opinion?

To form a composite picture of a man requires that we view him from many angles. To limn a religious portrait is no less a task. We

must look at Kennedy's public career, his relations with the clergy and individual lay people of many religious traditions, his understanding of the ineluctable tensions between church and state in American history, and some of his ethical and moral decisions. Then we should be able to draw some conclusions.

Structurally, this book begins with an examination of the "Catholic issue" in American politics from its inception to the eve of JFK's presidential campaign. It is impossible to understand the virulence of the religious issue in 1960 without some treatment of what Arthur Schlesinger called the oldest prejudice of the American people. Next, we shall relive the Kennedy campaign's handling of the religious issue and then look carefully at the way church-state conflicts were resolved during his brief presidency.

We shall then turn to an examination of the inner JFK and seek to ascertain the private religious side, seeing where his personal beliefs affected or shaped his public career. A comparison of Kennedy's "civil religion" with the pervasive "Presidential religion" of the Republic is also in order. We shall conclude with an examination of JFK's legacy to the nation, to the ecumenical movement, and to the Catholic community of which he was a loyal member.

In an appendix I have selected eight examples of public addresses or remarks which reflect on or reveal facets of Kennedy's religious life. I have placed each selection in historical context. With one exception they have never been reprinted since the text was originally issued. Taken cumulatively, they represent the major religious statements of Senator or President John F. Kennedy. They have never appeared in one place before.

Most of this book has been based on public records and both primary and secondary sources. In a few instances I have interviewed individuals intimately associated with our thirty-fifth president. Finally, I searched for every reference to religion in the papers and archives of the Kennedy Library in Waltham, Massachusetts. This valuable source, plus the many selections in the oral interview library, contribute to the authenticity of the study. All interpretations of the sources are, of course, my own. My appreciation to the staff of the Kennedy Library, and especially to Ms. Joan Hoopes, is hereby tendered. I am obviously indebted to my typists,

Mrs. Doris Black and Mrs. Sandra Aufrecht. My wife's encouragement and consistently valuable suggestions are also appreciated.

Albert J. Menendez
White Plains, New York

Notes

1. T.S. Settel, ed., *The Faith of John F. Kennedy* (New York: E.P. Dutton & Co., Inc., 1965), p. 5.

2. Lawrence B. Fuchs, *John F. Kennedy and American Catholicism* (Meredith Press, 1967), p. 73.

3. Robert McAfee Brown, *Christianity and Crisis*, 15 March 1959.

4. Quoted in Garry Wills, *Bare Ruined Choirs* (Garden City, NY: Doubleday, 1972).

5. Religious News Service, 14 June 1976.

6. Settel, *Faith of JFK*.

7. Ibid.

Chapter 1
THE CATHOLIC ISSUE IN AMERICAN POLITICS

Anti-Catholicism was part of the cultural baggage of the Protestant settlers in the British colonies that became the United States of America. The polemics that had begun with the Reformation had calcified into immobile positions on both sides of the Great Divide in Western Christendom. It was natural, then, that Protestants would carry a fear and hatred of the Church of Rome with them to the New World. Whether separatist Puritan, Scottish Presbyterian, or Cavalier Anglican, opposition to Rome was a touchstone of the Protestant mystique.

Although there were Catholics in the colonies, all were subject to vexatious discrimination. Even in Maryland, which had been founded as a refuge for British Catholics during the reign of Charles I, the soon outnumbered Catholics were subject to political and legal discrimination. Every colony maintained some form of legal harassment of "Papists" and many prohibited their very existence in the colony. Laws restricting public Catholic worship were commonplace. Priests were liable to arrest in Massachusetts. Catholics were excluded totally from public and political life, and in some states could not legally hold arms or educate their children. Not all of these laws were enforced. Some were ignored by temperate local authorities who had gotten to know their Catholic neigh-

bors and saw them as fellow human beings rather than as papal spies or conspirators.

Nevertheless, when outside forces seemed to threaten the security and placidity of the British colonies, Catholics were singled out for further discrimination. In Maryland they were subjected to a double tax and refused the right to bear arms. Catholics could not inherit land or estates. Mixed marriages had to be performed by Protestant clergy and, in the event of death of the Protestant partner, the children could be taken from the Catholic parent and placed in a Protestant family. Although rarely enforced, these were laws passed by Protestant legislatures.

In New York on August 15, 1741, two Catholics were executed, one woman being suspected of being a "professed Papist," and one clergyman accused of being a "Popish priest." It was discovered that he was a nonjuror High Episcopalian, but the discovery came too late for him! Catholics thus joined Quakers in the dubious role of martyrdom in colonial America.

After the passage of the Quebec Act by the British Parliament in 1763, a new wave of anti-Popery erupted. Charges were made that Britain was establishing a "sanguinary and impious" religion in the French colony adjoining British North America. Fears of papal aggression and invasion brought the level of discussion to the hysteria level. Harvard University maintained an annual anti-Catholic lecture, for which awards were given, and Guy Fawkes Day on November 5 was celebrated as an antipapal holy day in several colonies. (General George Washington later forbade the practice when he was commander in chief of the Continental Armies, calling it "childish, silly, and insulting.")

Catholics, though, were strong supporters of the revolution, and Charles Carroll of Maryland signed the Declaration of Independence. His cousin John Carroll was a friend of statesmen and a leading exponent of democracy in both church and state. He was elected the first Catholic bishop of the United States. There were only twenty-five to thirty thousand Catholics in the colonies in 1776, or well under one percent of the population.

Catholic growth was slow but unhindered and Catholics comprised only 1.9 percent of the population in 1800. Immigration

from Ireland and Germany increased, especially after 1840. Protestants feared even the slightest Catholic growth, and the famous Lyman Beecher delivered a sermon, "The Plea for the West," in which he warned Protestants to evangelize the Western parts of the continent to counteract growing Catholic influence. A number of Protestant organizations aimed their proselyting efforts toward the conversion of Catholic immigrant groups and were modestly successful in their efforts. "Up to 1820, the small, poor, and badly organized Catholic Church lost at least 250,000 followers to indifference or conversion, leaving no more than 200,000 practicing Catholics in the country."[1] There were 361,000 Catholics in 1830, but that figure rose to 1,614,000 in 1850, or 7 percent of the total population. Methodists, Baptists, and Presbyterians also increased their membership dramatically and together constituted 75 percent of all Protestants by 1850. Still, only 22 percent of all Americans were church members.

The first Catholic to serve in any Cabinet was appointed during this period. Roger Brooke Taney of Maryland was Andrew Jackson's Attorney General and Director of the Treasury and was later named to the Supreme Court, where he became the fifth Chief Justice.

Organized anti-Catholicism began in the 1830s and continued until the Civil War. Journalist Samuel F. B. Morse, in a series of pseudonymous newspaper articles and a book, *A Foreign Conspiracy Against the Liberties of the United States,* promoted the view that the Catholic countries of the Holy Alliance and the papacy were conspiring to subvert Protestant America. Religious extremism characterized this period, culminating in the burning of a Charleston, Massachusetts convent by a Protestant mob, and church burnings in Philadelphia in 1844. A flood of anti-Catholic literature and organizations is vividly described by historian Ray Allen Billington in his excellent book, *The Protestant Crusade, 1800-1860.* Bills were introduced in several state legislatures to restrict voting rights to native-born Protestants.

In the 1850s a group of extremists constituted themselves as the "Know-Nothing" (an accurate statement of their intellectual level) or Native American Party. They loathed Roman Catholics and

foreigners and were convinced that American institutions were Protestant to the core and would be jeopardized if Catholics were to hold public office.

In the 1852 campaign the Democrat, Franklin Pierce, of New Hampshire, was criticized by many Catholics because his state still maintained a test act against Catholic officeholders, which was not removed until 1902.

The Know-Nothings gained strength and were responsible for the mobbing of papal emissary Bedini when he toured the United States in 1853. In 1854 they did well in the congressional elections and swept local offices in Massachusetts, Delaware, Pennsylvania, Maryland, and Kentucky. Revision of immigration laws was a primary legislative goal, as were convent inspection bills. The increasing incidence of religious strife is symbolized by an occurrence in once tolerant Louisville. A Know-Nothing mayor had been elected in April 1855 and the *Louisville Journal* now saw Catholics as diabolical traitors and myrmidons of a foreign power. The paper urged Protestants to crush the Catholic threat on election day, August 6, 1855. Many voters took the warnings literally. As historian John Boles describes it:

Know-Nothing hoodlums patrolled the polls, "protecting" democracy from peacefully voting foreign-born citizens. Anger, fear, and frustration broke down better judgment, and the result was a day of terror. Mobs roamed the streets, assaulting German and Irish citizens. From a German ward came gunshots aimed toward nativists; a row of Irish homes were burned. Bullies were given license to maul, and both sides fought with abandon. Bishop Spalding gave the keys of the Catholic cathedral to the mayor, putting the burden of its protection on the civil authorities; otherwise much Catholic property might have been destroyed. When the furor finally subsided, twenty-two lay dead and countless others were wounded.[2]

In 1856 the Nativists ran former President Millard Fillmore, a Unitarian, for President. The newly formed Republican Party nominated the popular soldier-explorer John C. Fremont, who soon became the object of an absurd whispering campaign that he was a Catholic and that his daughter was educated in a convent. (He was an Episcopalian.) The Democrats nominated James Buchanan, of Pennsylvania, and adopted a platform blasting

religious prejudice. Buchanan won easily, Fremont did respectably well, sweeping much of the North, and Fillmore carried only Maryland. Division among the Nativists over slavery overshadowed the religious issue. The movement vanished, only to reappear under new names and leaders in the 1890s.

The Civil War tended to mitigate religious prejudice and no religious issues appeared in the 1860, 1864, and 1868 elections. By the 1870s the contentious issue of public aid to religious schools brought about a rebirth of Protestant-Catholic antagonism.

Attempts were made to outlaw any aid to church schools by a constitutional amendment proposed by James G. Blaine, and it very nearly passed. Republican candidates and platforms endorsed the "Blaine Amendment," while Democrats, relying strongly on Catholic support, remained neutral.

In 1884 came the celebrated slogan, "Rum, Romanism, and Rebellion." The Republican nominee was James G. Blaine, "the plumed knight" (as atheist orator Robert Ingersoll called him in his nominating speech). Blaine had been a U.S. Senator, Speaker of the House, and Secretary of State. Born of a Presbyterian father and an Irish Catholic mother and raised a Catholic, he had become a Presbyterian in adulthood. This, plus his antiparochiaid amendment, was bound to alienate many Catholic voters. However, Blaine, whose cousin was mother superior of a convent, refused to countenance any criticism of his mother's faith. On the other hand, Grover Cleveland, the Democratic candidate, was not particularly popular among Catholics. The usually Democratic Catholic vote was up for grabs.

Extraneous nonsense abounded. Blaine was accused of educating one of his daughters in a convent in Paris, while allowing another daughter to be married by a "Romish priest" to a former officer of the Papal Guards.

In late October a weary Blaine attended a fund-raising dinner in New York City. On the morning of October 29 at the Park Avenue Hotel, several hundred Protestant clergymen gathered to hear the candidate. They selected Rev. Samuel D. Burchard, a Presbyterian, as chairman and asked him to make a short welcoming statement. In it he said: "We expect to vote for you next Tuesday. We are Republicans and don't propose to leave our party and identify

ourselves with the party whose antecedents have been rum, Romanism, and rebellion." Journalists present apparently did not hear the offensive statement or did not consider it significant. However, a shorthand reporter, sent by the Democratic Party, recorded the statement. Within days handbills were placed in Roman Catholic parishes throughout the East. Blaine called the comment "exceedingly unfortunate," but his disclaimer probably came too late.

Blaine narrowly lost New York by 1,149 votes and, thus, the election. Whether the intemperate remark of the partisan preacher played a role in the voters' decision is problematic. There were no public opinion polls and almost no viable data on which to analyze religious voting in those days. Some scholars, like historian De Santis, believed that "the importance of this incident in causing Blaine's defeat has been exaggerated."[3]

The American Protective Association (APA), the newest anti-Catholic group, was organized in Clinton, Iowa, in 1887. Its avowedly political aims were to oppose any Catholic candidates or Catholic political influence. The APA specialized in bogus papal encyclicals and lurid scare stories about arsenals in Catholic cathedrals, convents, churches, and schools. Virtual hysteria erupted in isolated rural areas where gossip was gospel. The APA proved to be something of a flash in the pan, for, though it carried many communities in Nebraska, Iowa, Illinois, Michigan, and Ohio in 1892 and 1894, it soon dissipated and vanished from the political scene. Where it was a factor, it tended to work with and be absorbed by the Republican Party.

In 1888 appeared a shocking book, *Washington in the Lap of Rome*, by Boston Baptist preacher Justin Dewey Fulton. Fulton was a longtime critic of Rome and author of a previous shocker, *Why Priests Should Wed*, which barely escaped prosecution under the Comstock antiobscenity law. Fulton charged that "Romanism is the dominant power in the Capitol of the United States. Lincoln, Grant, and Arthur withstood it, and suffered the consequences. The power is unseen. It is shadowy. It inhabits the air and infects it. Romanism is the malaria of the spiritual world. It stupefies the brain, deadens the heart, and sears the conscience as with a hot iron." Fulton also charged that Roman Catholics had assassinated Lincoln, a refrain often repeated in the anti-Catholic underground.

In 1892 a minor religious issue caused some strife. The Catholic Church had been the primary educator of many Indians in the western states, and its Indian reservation schools received some public funding under a contract of 1869. Under this arrangement the church furnished buildings, board, lodging, and clothing for the students, and the government allowed a fixed annual per capita compensation. The Bureau of Catholic Indian Missions acted as liaison with the government. Although the project began under a Republican administration, Democrat Grover Cleveland increased federal appropriations from $65,220 in 1884 to $347,672 in 1889. The Presbyterians, who maintained a few schools, received $41,825. The Republican Presidential victory of 1888 augured some changes.

President Benjamin Harrison named General Thomas J. Morgan, a Baptist minister, to the post of Indian commissioner, and Dr. Daniel Dorchester, a noted Methodist preacher and author, to the position of Commissioner of Indian Education. Morgan promptly announced that he would withdraw government aid from the religious schools. Morgan then dismissed Catholics who were serving in the Indian office. Dorchester, who had written a savage book *Romanism Versus the Public School System* in 1888, fired almost all Catholic teachers. Catholics were outraged but were unable to reverse the policies.

Harry J. Sievers believes that this issue "resulted in an apparently heavy Catholic vote against President Harrison in 1892."[4] Harrison was defeated by ex-President Cleveland, and much of the Catholic press exulted. *The Courier* of Ogdensburg, New York, declared it "a great Catholic victory," and the *Catholic Herald* of New York remarked: "The Republican Party, led by bigots, invaded the sanctuary of the home, usurped parental rights, and robbed the Catholic Indians of their only treasure, their faith; but the people, true to the best traditions of America, hurled it from power. Cleveland's victory was, in truth, the defeat of bigotry."

Historian De Santis places the Civil War elections in historical perspective. "Catholicism was dragged into practically every presidential election in the post-Civil War generation. Yet as an issue it played a minor and subordinate role, and never came close to being a determining factor in the outcome of any one of these contests."[5]

The Spanish American War brought Catholicism to the fore as a political issue once again. Since Spain was a Catholic bastion, many Protestants thought that American Catholics would be unwilling to fight against Spain. Archbishop John Ireland, a personal friend of President McKinley, was asked by the Vatican to try and convince the president not to declare war on Spain. He tried valiantly for two weeks, but, when war was declared, Ireland, who had endorsed McKinley in 1896, called upon American Catholics to accept the war effort and contribute to its success.

After the war, though, the American seizure of Cuba, Puerto Rico, and the Philippine Islands was viewed as an imperialistic land-grab. Furthermore, these were almost completely Catholic nations, and Protestant missionaries seized the opportunity to "invade" them. President McKinley inadvertently insulted American Catholics by claiming that one of the reasons for the annexation of the Philippines was "to Christianize" the natives. This naïve view angered Catholics, who reminded the President that there were Christians in the islands three hundred years before there were any in Ohio.

Protestant militants saw the Americanization as an opening wedge to the Protestantization, beginning with mass distribution of the Protestant Bible and the opening of Protestant schools and colleges. As Thomas E. Wangler points out: "Some Protestants interpreted the new expansionism of the nation as a providentially arranged opportunity to spread a purified, reformed religion to savage peoples kept ignorant by Catholic governments and priests."[6]

Archbishop Ireland interceded with Presidents McKinley and Roosevelt to name a Catholic to the Peace Commission, to rescind the civil marriage law in Cuba, and to select Catholic teachers for the Filipino public schools. This pleased Catholics without angering Protestants unduly, since the latter were pleased with the progress they were making in the heavily Catholic lands. In addition, William Howard Taft, the newly named civil governor negotiated a sensitive settlement of expropriated friars' lands with the Vatican. The delicacy of the church-state negotiations in this conflict showed that American domestic politics could both affect and be affected by foreign policy questions and religious conflicts.[7]

Woodrow Wilson was free from religious questioning, though some fundamentalists attacked his appointment of Louis Brandeis, the first Jewish Supreme Court justice, and his meeting with Pope Benedict XV at the Vatican during his triumphal tour of Europe.

On Thanksgiving Day, 1915, on the top of Stone Mountain, near Atlanta, Georgia, the infamous Knights of the Ku Klux Klan was reconstituted. Its bêtes noires were Catholics, Jews, and Negroes. It was sworn to uphold Anglo-Saxon Protestant civilization. The Invisible Empire soon grew to frightening strength and disgraced American life for decades to come. By 1924 it was reliably estimated to have 4 or 5 million members, being strongest in Indiana, Ohio, and Texas. Considerable support was given the Klan by Protestant clergy. Of the 39 "national lecturers" employed by the Klan from 1922 to 1928, 26 were Protestant ministers. Of 241 pamphleteers and agitators used by the Klan, 110 were preachers.[8]

Other anti-Catholic militants included the Guardians of Liberty, founded by Georgia politician Tom Watson, who spewed forth a torrent of bigotry from his Jeffersonian Publishing Company in Thomson, Georgia; the Knights of Luther; the *Menace*, published in Aurora, Missouri, and claiming over one million readers in its heyday; the Rail Splitter Press in Milan, Illinois, under the aegis of the redoubtable William Lloyd Clark, who called himself "an anti-Papal propagandist"; the Protestant Guards of Washington, D.C.; and *The Protestant*, a monthly journal founded by Gilbert O. Nations, Ph.D., a scholarly sophisticated bigot who sought the Presidency in 1924 and wrote such books as *Rome in Congress* and *Roman Catholic War on Public Schools*.

There was a mild religious boom, oddly enough, during the jazz age. Presbyterians, Lutherans, and Baptists gained over a million new members between 1916 and 1926. Episcopalians almost doubled from 1.1 million to 1.9 million. The feared Roman Catholic Church increased from 15.7 to 18.6 million.

The morbid fears of anti-Catholic agitators about growing Catholic political power in the 1920s is not substantiated by sober fact. Although Catholics then constituted 16 percent of the population, there were almost no Catholics in the Republican cabinets or high judiciary appointments. There were few Catholic governors. A survey by Dr. Charles E. Jefferson, a foremost Congregational-

ist pastor, found only thirty-eight Catholics in the House of Representatives in 1924, a figure representing less than 9 percent of the members.[9]

Nevertheless, Dr. Gilbert Nations warned in *Rome in Congress* that Catholics were about to seize effective political control of the United States. In 1927 the Fellowship Forum published a lurid and silly expose, *Proof of Rome's Political Meddling in America*, which charged that Catholics controlled the bureaucracy and Congress. It came complete with maps showing "the strategic location of important Roman Catholic institutions which almost surround all of the important government buildings." The book failed to deliver. It turned out to be an exhaustive and rather boring study of the National Catholic Welfare Conference and its activities as a religious lobby. An intricate organizational chart made the book almost suitable for a college government class, but hardly demonstrated a convincing case of an imminent papal coup d'etat.

The candidacy of Alfred E. Smith provoked interfaith tensions as no other previous campaign had done. Smith, whose forebears came from Ireland, was born on the Lower East Side of New York in 1873. His formal education ended before he completed the ninth grade, when he had to quit school to help support his family. He had a natural inclination for politics and soon entered into its rough-and-tumble arena in New York City. In 1904 he was elected to the New York State Assembly and served there until 1915. He later became sheriff of New York County, president of the board of aldermen of New York City, and governor of New York in 1918. He was defeated in the Republican landslide of 1920, but reelected in 1922, 1924, and 1926. His record was considered relatively progressive and much in tune with the needs of his urban constituents.

His record on religious affairs was somewhat mixed. In 1915 he offered an amendment to the Commissioner of Education at the New York State Constitutional Convention that would have eliminated the state ban on aid to parochial schools. As governor he continued the practice of supplying four million dollars a year in state aid to parochial schools. He was also somewhat naïve about the public relations consequences of his public religious life. He made several well-publicized trips to the Vatican, where Pope Pius XI effusively praised him. He had a picture of Pope Pius XI

hanging in the governor's mansion in Albany, and he made an appearance at the 1926 Eucharistic Congress in Chicago, where he is supposed to have kissed a cardinal's ring, provoking an angry outburst from Methodist Bishop Adna W. Leonard, who said, "No governor can kiss the papal ring and get within gun shot of the White House."[10]

On the other hand, Smith appointed excellent men to the state cabinet, including a reasonable balance of Protestants, Catholics, and Jews. He approved a bill entending the grounds for divorce, which the Catholic Church opposed. He objected to most forms of public censorship, though he signed the so-called Padlock Bill of 1927, which provided for the closing of any theaters for an entire year if any play presented was declared indecent by the courts. He also reorganized state government and supported social welfare and public education. He denounced the Lusk Committee, which was an early un-American activities committee seeking Communists in the New York state government. He won the admiration of many liberals and intellectuals.

In a sense the 1928 campaign began in 1924, as Smith was one of the two leading contenders for the Democratic Presidential nomination. His opponent was former Secretary of the Treasury William G. McAdoo, who represented the Protestant-prohibitionist rural wing of the party. Smith represented the urban antiprohibitionist and largely Catholic and Jewish segments of the party. The Democratic convention was so bitterly divided that it narrowly defeated a resolution condemning the Ku Klux Klan and then could not make up its mind whether to nominate Smith or McAdoo. On the 103rd ballot, the weary delegates finally settled on a dull, colorless Wall Street lawyer from West Virginia, John W. Davis. The liberals were angry at the party's failure to break with the Bryan-populist tradition and deserted the party in droves to support the candidacy of "Fighting Bob" La Follette of Wisconsin. The Democrats received the lowest vote in their entire history—less than 29 percent of the national total—and carried no states outside of the South. Smith was reelected governor of New York handily and began preparing for the 1928 campaign.

The first serious discussion of the religious issue arose in 1927, when Charles C. Marshall, a scholarly Episcopalian lawyer and a

self-proclaimed admirer of the Roman Catholic Church, published his "Open Letter to Governor Alfred E. Smith" in the April 1927 issue of *Atlantic Monthly*. Marshall had spent years studying Catholicism and professed a "love for the Latin church." Nevertheless he was seriously concerned about Vatican policy on the relationship of church and state and its historic hostility to religious liberty. Did such policies demand a dual loyalty among prospective Roman Catholic public servants in a democratic, non-Catholic society? He questioned whether Smith could be sufficiently independent of the various papal encyclicals on church-state relations. He worried about whether religious harmony and peace could be preserved if there were constant church-state antagonisms. It was a thoughtful and serious article and Governor Smith agreed to reply in the May 1927 issue of the same journal.

Smith, who is alleged to have said after reading Marshall's article, "What the hell is a papal encyclical?" (revealing his rather limited knowledge of Catholicism), asked Father Patrick Duffy, the famous World War I chaplain, and a young priest, Francis J. Spellman, later to become cardinal, to help him prepare a response. Smith's response did not really answer most of the questions Marshall raised but pledged that he was a loyal American, a genuine patriot, and a true Catholic at the same time. He professed strong support for separation of church and state and public education. He wrote: "I believe in the support of the public school as one of the cornerstones of American liberty. I believe in the right of every parent to choose whether his child shall be educated in the public school or in a religious school, supported by those of his own faith."

Unfortunately, this was to be the only rational discussion of the religious issue for the next year and a half. Most Roman Catholics objected to Smith's even being asked to respond to Marshall, and most Roman Catholic periodicals refused to discuss the issues Marshall raised. On the other hand, Protestant extremists refused to accept Smith's guarantee of good faith and began a long campaign to preserve their dominance over American public life and to keep the White House closed to Roman Catholics.

Although Smith had written in his *Atlantic Monthly* article that he recognized "no power in the institutions of my church to inter-

fere with the operations of the Constitution of the United States or the enforcement of the law of the land," millions of Protestants refused to believe him. When Smith had written, "I believe in absolute freedom of conscience for all men and in equality of all churches, all sects, and all beliefs before the law as a matter of right and not as a matter of favor," Protestants pointed to papal encyclicals that said just the opposite.

Much of the religious issue was sub rosa. Edmund Moore has written that "anti-Catholicism was indeed the silent issue in the national press and was very much more significant than the somewhat meager news or editorial space assigned to it would indicate."[11] Senator Tom Heflin of Alabama, a frock-coated demagogue, made violent anti-Catholic speeches on the floor of Congress.

The Protestant churches were politicized as never before, and almost all religious periodicals warned of the alleged dangers to religious freedom if Smith were elected.

The Republican Party was not completely immune from occasionally indulging in some anti-Catholicism for political gain. Mrs. Willie W. Caldwell, a Virginia National Committeewoman, wrote to the women in her state, saying: "Mr. Hoover himself and the National Committee are depending on the women to save our country in this hour of very vital moral religious crisis. We must save the United States from being Romanized and rum-ridden, and the call is to the women to do something." Her letter outraged many Democrats and liberal Republicans. Republican officials in Florida and North Carolina distributed anti-Catholic literature. Perhaps the worst violator was Mrs. Mabel Walker Willebrandt, an assistant attorney general assigned to Prohibition enforcement. On September 7, she spoke to a delegation of Methodists in the Ohio Methodist Conference in Springfield, Ohio, and made a none-too-subtle appeal for religious bloc votes. She said: "There are two thousand pastors here. You have in your churches more than six hundred thousand members of the Methodist Church in Ohio alone. That is enough to swing the election."[12]

To his credit, Republican nominee Herbert Hoover denounced the Caldwell letter and made some appeals for religious harmony. In his memoirs published after the campaign, however, Hoover

blamed Smith for introducing the religious issue in the public arena by Smith's famous September 20 address before a rather hostile crowd in Oklahoma City. This seems rather absurd of Hoover, since the religious issue was the most emotional and most widely discussed issue in the entire campaign. Smith faced the crowd at Oklahoma City and lashed out at his enemies as bigots. He said that no one had a right to question his religion, that he was a loyal and patriotic American, and that his cabinet had had ten Protestants, one Jew, and only three Catholics. He talked about "the wicked motive of religious intolerance" and said that "no decent right-minded, upstanding American citizen can for a moment countenance the shower of lying statements, with no basis in fact, that has been reduced to printed matter and sent broadcast through the mails of this country." Smith went on to say: "I here emphatically declare that I do not wish any member of my faith in any part of the United States to vote for me on any religious grounds. I want them to vote for me only when in their hearts and consciences they become convinced that my election will promote the best interests of our country. By the same token, I cannot refrain from saying that any person who votes against me simply because of my religion is not, to my way of thinking, a good citizen. Let me remind the Democrats of this country that we belong to the party of Thomas Jefferson, whose proudest boast was that he was the author of the Virginia Statute for Religious Freedom. Let me remind the citizens of every political faith that his Statute of Religious Freedom has become a part of the sacred heritage of our land."[13]

Smith's appeal, reinforced by the support of some liberal Protestant, Jewish, and Episcopalian religious leaders, came to no avail. The passionate religious antagonisms of the past were insurmountable. Smith went down to a crushing defeat, 21.4 to 15.0 million in the popular vote and 444-87 in electoral votes. He made substantial gains in Catholic and Jewish areas, carrying Massachusetts, Rhode Island, and most major urban areas, but he lost badly in the heartland of rural, southern, and western Protestantism. Richard Hofstadter writes: "Even in his losing campaign Smith turned the normally huge Republican pluralities in the twelve largest cities into a slender Democratic plurality. He brought into the voting stream

of the Democratic Party ethnic groups that had never taken part in politics and others that had been mainly Republican. He extricated his party from its past dependence on agrarian interests and made it known to the great urban populations. He lost a campaign that had to be lost, but in such a way as to restore his party as an effective opposition and to pave the way for the victories of F.D.R.''[14]

In retrospect, Smith and his advisers were not completely blameless in the way they handled the religious issue. Smith appointed John J. Raskob, a conservative Catholic millionaire from Delaware, as chairman of the Democratic National Committee. It probably would have been wiser to have appointed a more neutral figure, but Smith was apparently unaware of the deep suspicion with which he was regarded. David Burner expresses a view that is more widely accepted today: "For if he could not shirk his religion itself, or modify the slightest symbolic act of allegiance, he could have at least addressed himself more fully to the fears in which so many of his fellow Americans had been reared .... Smith might have acknowledged the occasional alliance between Latin Catholicism and political tyranny and then pointed to the historical American tradition of religious harmony, as embodied in Lord Baltimore; he and his supporters might even have made explicit contrast between their position, along with the position of countless of their fellow religionists in the United States, and that of Catholic reactionaries; he might have sought out the support of Protestant clergymen or outstanding laymen; he might have increased the Protestant contingent in his campaign committee. In short, Smith might have acted as though he was aware of the anxiety, however silly or bigoted, that was felt by much of rural American Protestantism, as one who shared with it a sense of America's role in preserving religious liberty."[15] Dr. James H. Smylie, in his trenchant essay, "The Roman Catholic Church, The State and Al Smith" (*Church History*, September 1960), found a kernel of hopefulness in the rather unfortunate campaign. "Roman Catholics were slandered; of this there is no shadow of a doubt. But there is evidence that Roman Catholics themselves invited, indeed, provoked, in their own writings a discussion of the relationship between the church and the state in America. During the 1928 cam-

paign, some Americans raised questions about the feasibility of a Roman Catholic president in an attempt to come to terms with one of the most crucial and continuing problems in American life.''

Another lesson of that sorry campaign is expressed by Eleanor Roosevelt. ''The kind of propaganda that some of the religious groups, aided and abetted by the opposition, put forth in that campaign utterly disgusted me. If I needed anything to show me what prejudice can do to the intelligence of human beings, that campaign was the best lesson I could have had.''[16]

American Catholics strongly favored FDR in 1932. His denunciation of religious bigotry in the 1928 campaign, his signing of the Love-Hayes Bill, which prohibited religious tests for public school teachers in New York, and even his quoting of a papal encyclical in an October 2, 1932 speech in Detroit endeared him to Catholic voters.[17]

The election of FDR brought a new day for America's Catholics and Jews, both of whom had been excluded from direct participation in the country's political life by the Protestant Establishment. Until FDR only four Catholics had served in the cabinet in one hundred forty years. From 1897 to 1922 the only Catholics to hold high appointive office were Supreme Court Justices Joseph McKenna and Pierce Butler. Only 4 percent of federal judgeships went to Catholics in the Republican 1920s, and even Democrat Woodrow Wilson had no Catholics in his cabinet. This was to change under Roosevelt.

FDR selected Montana's progressive Senator Thomas Walsh as attorney general, but Walsh died on the train taking him to Washington to accept the appointment. Frank Murphy, another Catholic, was named to replace him. Murphy was later named to the U.S. Supreme Court. James A. Farley, chairman of the Democratic National Committee, became Postmaster General and Joseph P. Kennedy, chairman of the Securities and Exchange Commission. About 25 percent of federal judiciary appointments went to Catholics under FDR and his successor Harry Truman. FDR was the first President to have two Catholics in his cabinet at the same time. Strangely enough, many conservatively inclined Catholic Democrats grew disillusioned by FDR's foreign policy and turned bitterly against the President. Catholics opposed the recog-

nition of Soviet Russia and continued U. S. support for an anti-clerical regime in Mexico. The Catholic press and high clergy sought to change those policies. The celebrated radio preacher, Father Charles Coughlin, led the attacks beginning in 1935. Even Al Smith bolted the party, supported the Liberty League and Republican candidate Alf Landon in 1936.

FDR's appointment of Myron Taylor as personal representative or "ambassador extraordinary" to the Vatican on December 24, 1939 angered Protestant opinion and resulted "in the deterioration of the good relations between the churches."[18] Although FDR insisted that the "motive for the appointment was the advancement of world peace," Protestant leaders, especially Baptists, Methodists, and Lutherans, deplored the appointment and urged its cancellation several times during the 1940s.[19] FDR felt it necessary to meet with ten Protestant churchmen at the White House on January 9, 1940. They were still unconvinced, and the Vatican's announcement that Taylor would be considered a full ambassador stiffened Protestant opposition. The Southern Baptist Convention repeatedly denounced the appointment in its annual meetings.[20]

The Catholic issue worked both ways. James A. Farley decided to seek the Presidency in 1940 before FDR had made up his mind to run for a third term. A Gallup survey found that 61 percent would vote for a well-qualified Catholic but a large 30 percent would not—a considerable hurdle for any prospective Catholic nominee. Political leaders reacted negatively and the boomlet for Farley died.[21] In 1944 James Byrnes of South Carolina was vetoed as FDR's running mate because, as a young man, he had switched from the Roman Catholic Church to the Episcopal Church.[22] The same thing happened to New Jersey Governor Robert Meyner in 1956. He was considered a prospective running mate for Stevenson until it was noted that he, too, was an ex-Catholic become Episcopalian.

On a personal level Protestant-Catholic relations generally improved during the depression and the war years, though the official institutional churches were still quite aloof and distrustful of each other. The Roman Catholic Church continued to gain in membership and in corresponding political and social influence. Buttressed by many notable conversions, it progressed substantially

"to make America Catholic." Protestants were wary and rather uncertain of the ultimate goals of their traditional rival.

A deterioration in relationships began after World War II. Protestants accused the Roman Catholic hierarchy of placing pressure on the U.S. State Department to deny visas to Protestant missionaries to South America. Repeated harassment of Protestants in such Catholic lands as Spain and Colombia added to the distrust. The Vatican officially frowned on the burgeoning ecumenical movement, rejecting Catholic participation on any official level. It refused to send Catholic delegates to the inaugural sessions of the World Council of Churches in Amsterdam in 1948. Papal encyclicals, beginning especially with *Mortalium Animos* (1928, Pius XI), called on Protestants, Anglicans, and Orthodox heretics and schismatics to return to the ancient mother church of Christendom.

Furthermore, Roman Catholics were demanding public aid for their schools and hospitals as a matter of distributive justice and fair public policy, thus creating a new wedge in interfaith relationships. Paul Blanshard's provocative and widely read *American Freedom and Catholic Power* articulated the deep-rooted fears of many Protestants and liberals. John Cogley, then a liberal Catholic journalist, admits in his *Catholic America* that "over the years there were enough examples of the use of Catholic power to unsettle any liberal dedicated to freedom of thought and expression who might be uncertain about the Church's ultimate aims. ... The liberals' case against Catholicism was founded on solid fact and easy to document."[23]

A Catholic bishops' 1948 pastoral letter referred to separation of church and state as "a shibboleth of doctrinaire secularism."

In hotly contested referenda in Massachusetts in 1946 and 1948, organized Catholic efforts successfully maintained a legal ban on birth control. Against what was perceived as a militant and aggressive policy of proselytism and political influence, Protestants and Other Americans United was organized as a counterforce.

Catholics countered by claiming that they had a constitutional right to seek both expanding political influence and larger church membership. They claimed that much of contemporary Protestantism was dessicated, devoid of spiritual authority and certainty. One of their spokesmen, James M. O'Neill, in his *Catholicism and*

American Freedom, acquitted Catholics of the charges made by Blanshard. He contended that Catholicism's emphasis on authority independent of the state would strengthen democracy and freedom and prevent socialism and communism. O'Neill also maintained that Catholic members of Congress and the Catholic electorate in general were divided along conservative-liberal and Democratic-Republican lines just like the other religions and did not constitute a disloyal clericalist bloc.

Some Protestants expressed fear and dismay about growing Catholic influence in Washington, and Southern Baptists even raged against sending U.S. representatives to the funeral of Pope Pius XI in 1939. A typical Baptist viewpoint was expressed by the Georgia Baptist weekly.

The stranglehold which the Vatican has gradually gained in Washington is now manifest at every crossroads in the country, save in the South and in certain sections of the West. There is not a politician in the country who does not keep an ear to the ground to see which way Cardinal Spellman is nodding. Millions upon millions of money, much of it garnered from evangelical Christians' pockets, is being poured into concrete foundations for an institution of America under direct and ancient Romanized patterns. The constant flow of foreign-born people into our country, most of them traditional subjects of Rome, plus the intelligent and aggressive missionary programs amongst the Negroes, the rural areas, and, as always, in the urban centers, is daily adding to the strength of the hierarchy in our country.[24]

Catholics were indeed gaining some political influence, but hardly enough to justify such apocalyptic statements.

A 1948 survey found Catholics a poor second to Methodists in Congress, holding 77 seats to the Methodists' 112. The Catholic figure was under 15 percent, still an underrepresentation. This Congress was the Republican landslide Congress of 1946, so Catholic representation was a shade below the Roosevelt years. There were only 7 Jews, a figure lower than in the 1920s and 1930s, for some strange reason.[25] Another survey of the governors that year found only one Catholic governor out of 48.[26]

President Harry S. Truman's decision to appoint Mark W. Clark as official U.S. ambassador to the Vatican on October 20, 1951, rather than as a personal representative (as FDR had done with

Myron C. Taylor) provoked an unexpected fury from the Protestant community. Protestants charged that such an action would give preferential treatment to Catholicism and would violate the spirit, if not the letter, of the First Amendment. Mass protest meetings and a nationwide letter writing campaign to Congress and the White House were so intense that General Clark, an Episcopalian, asked that his name be withdrawn on January 13, 1952. One sidelight to this nasty controversy was President Truman's pique at his personal pastor's sermon (Dr. Edward Hughes Pruden of Washington's First Baptist Church) against the appointment. Truman intensely disliked meddling clerics and he never returned to services at First Baptist.

Most of the controversy was vituperative, though at least one scholar, Mark DeWolfe Howe of Harvard Law School, challenged the constitutionality of the appointment in his article "Diplomacy, Religion and the Constitution" (*Nation,* January 12, 1952). Edwin S. Corwin of Princeton University and Arthur M. Schlesinger, Jr., of Harvard supported the nomination and ridiculed the opposition as nativists. "On the whole," writes F. William O'Brien, "the secular press was favorably disposed toward having an American ambassador at the Vatican."[27] The *New York Times* and the *Washington Post* editorially endorsed the Truman appointment.

The National Council of Churches and the National Association of Evangelicals (NAE) vigorously opposed the nomination. The NAE sent petitions to eight thousand churches on Reformation Sunday and reported spending $500,000 on radio time in three days in late October 1951. The *Christian Century* (October 31, 1951) warned senators that their vote on Clark's confirmation "will play a decisive role" in their political future. Methodist Bishop G. Bromley Oxnam even predicted in an Akron, Ohio, address that the Vatican ambassadorship "may well determine the 1952 election." A Congregationalist pastor in Milwaukee, Rev. Stoddard Patterson, told his congregation to "vote for Protestants at the polls—Protestants who will uphold the Protestant traditions."

The Catholic press supported the appointment on the grounds that the United States had a reliable ally in the Vatican in the struggle with world communism. Most Catholic spokesmen, though, clerical and lay, expressed dismay at the Protestant out-

burst and almost seemed willing to let the whole issue go away rather than to reawaken interfaith animosities.

Protestants won a major victory, so it seems, in this battle, though not without some eyebrow raising at the methods engaged in by some of their leaders. *Christianity and Crisis* (November 26, 1951) chided their fellow Protestants and said that many "seem so guided by emotion that they make a poor choice of issues for major emphasis." A nasty dispute in the late 1940s between Mrs. Eleanor Roosevelt and Francis Cardinal Spellman, the unofficial U.S. primate, over the question of public aid for parochial schools symbolized to many the growing divergence between liberal democracy and official Catholicism. The vehemence of the cardinal's attack on the revered widow of a beloved President shocked many Americans. His hat-in-hand apology at Hyde Park amused and relieved all but the most reactionary haters of Mrs. Roosevelt.

Protestant-Catholic relations were still strained through the 1950s, though more Catholics were elected to public office in non-Catholic strongholds (Edmund Muskie in Maine, Eugene McCarthy in Minnesota, etc.). Hostility to a Catholic President, which stood at 30 percent or more in polls throughout the 1940s and 1950s, declined to 25 percent in 1958 (34 percent among Protestants said that they would vote against a Catholic nominee of their party).

In 1956 two leading Roman Catholics, Massachusetts Senator John F. Kennedy and New York Mayor Robert F. Wagner, were considered strong contenders for the Democratic vice-presidential nomination, after presidential aspirant Adlai E. Stevenson threw the vice-presidential nomination open to convention delegates. A secret "memorandum" prepared by Connecticut Democrat John Bailey was circulated among many party officials in an attempt to secure the nomination for a Catholic.[28] It contended that millions of Catholic Democrats who liked Dwight D. Eisenhower in 1952 would return to the party if a Catholic were chosen as Stevenson's running mate. It was especially significant that Catholics were overwhelmingly concentrated in large population states with correspondingly large electoral votes. *U.S. News & World Report* summarized the essence of the Bailey argument as follows: "If he brought into the Democratic fold only those normally Democratic

Catholics who voted for Ike, he could probably swing New York, Massachusetts, Rhode Island, Connecticut, Pennsylvania and Illinois—for 132 electoral votes. If he also wins the votes of Catholics who shifted to the Republicans in 1948 or earlier, he could also swing New Jersey, Minnesota, Michigan, California, Wisconsin, Ohio, Maryland, Montana, and maybe even New Hampshire—for a total of 265 electoral votes (needed to win: 266). Thus Ike could and would be defeated.''[29]

When this strategy was revealed, the leading Protestant journal *Christian Century* (August 15, 1956) erupted with uncharacteristic ardor. "The Roman Catholic Church is not reconciled to those aspects of the Constitution of the United States, and in particular of the First Amendment, which keep Church and State separate, make illegal the use of tax money for the support of religious establishments and insist that all churches shall stand on equal footing in their relation to the State." The journal opposed Wagner and Kennedy because neither "has demonstrated sufficient independence so that he can be trusted to stand against the never ceasing drive of the Roman Catholic Church for access to public funds ... and for preferential treatment by public figures and bodies."

Kennedy narrowly lost the nomination to Tennessee Senator Estes Kefauver, a sentimental favorite, but enthusiastically campaigned for the ticket. (JFK had placed Stevenson's name in nomination.) Eisenhower received a record Catholic vote for a Republican (49 percent in Gallup, 53 percent in the University of Michigan survey), but there is no evidence that failure to nominate Kennedy had anything to do with it. Foreign policy issues and the personal charisma of Eisenhower were the dominant reasons.

The 1958 election was a dress rehearsal for the public raising of the religious issue in 1960. The issue arose primarily in two states, California and Pennsylvania. In California a referendum on tax exemption of parochial school property was the occasion for an outpouring of verbal hostility to Catholicism. Catholic schools were called "unAmerican" in the literature of the forces promoting "Proposition 16," to deny tax exemption. The usual anti-Catholic smears were prominent. I personally examined the materials on file

at the Fair Campaign Practices Committee (FCPC) in Washington and it is my conclusion that the Proposition 16 forces were mostly dishonest and unfair in their tactics. They were opposed by many church-state separationists and political and religious liberals, including Episcopal Bishop James Pike. Lutherans, Seventh-day Adventists, and Episcopalians opposed the measure. It was decisively rejected.

During the same election California Attorney General Edmund Brown, the Democratic gubernatorial nominee and a Roman Catholic, was denounced by fundamentalists because he had ruled against obligatory Bible readings in public schools. The old canards about Catholic hatred of the Bible were bandied about in some of the extremist religious press. Since Brown defeated his Republican opponent, Senator William Knowland, by a 60 percent to 40 percent vote landslide, the religious issue certainly must not have hurt him substantially. He won the Protestant Central Valley as well as the urban Catholic and Jewish areas.

In Pennsylvania, however, Pittsburgh Mayor David Lawrence's Catholicism almost cost him the election for governor. A widely respected Stevensonian liberal, Lawrence was heavily favored to defeat a Republican nonentity, businessman Arthur McGonigle, who had never held public office. Pennsylvania had never had a Catholic governor, and the rural Protestant Bible Belt reacted with a vengeance. Though Lawrence won, by fewer than one hundred thousand votes out of almost four million cast, his victory came from the Catholic, Jewish, and more liberal Protestant urban and suburban areas. Lawrence ran poorly in the Protestant strongholds that had buried Al Smith under an avalanche in 1928.

The FCPC, in a September 1959 memorandum, concluded that there had been a shocking increase in anti-Catholicism in the 1958 election. The FCPC was organized in 1954 to fight political chicanery and dishonest campaign tactics. Under the leadership of executive director Bruce L. Felknor and chairman Charles P. Taft, it was especially sensitive to religious and racial smears.

Despite the escalating bias, five new Catholic governors and eight new U.S. Senators were elected in the 1958 Democratic sweep.

Notes

1. Lawrence B. Fuchs, *John F. Kennedy and American Catholicism* (Meredith Press, 1967), p. 73.

2. John B. Boles, *Religion in Antebellum Kentucky,* Bicentennial Bookshelf Series (Lexington, KY: Univ. Press of Kentucky, 1976), p. 78.

3. Vincent P. De Santis, "Catholicism and Presidential Elections, 1865-1900," *Mid-America*, April 1960.

4. Harry J. Sievers, "The Catholic Indian School Issue and the Presidential Election of 1892," *Catholic Historical Review*, July 1952.

5. De Santis, "Catholicism and Presidential Elections."

6. Thomas E. Wangler, "American Catholics and the Spanish-American War," in *Catholics in America 1776-1976*, ed. Robert Trisco (Washington: National Conference of Catholic Bishops, 1976).

7. Frank T. Reuter, *Catholic Influence on American Colonial Policies 1898-1904* (Austin, TX: University of Texas Press, 1967).

8. Michael Williams, *The Shadow of the Pope* (Whittlesey House, 1932), pp. 317-318; see also, Thomas M. Conroy, "The Ku Klux Klan and the American Clergy," *American Ecclesiastical Review,* January 1924.

9. Everett Ross Clinchy, *All In the Name of God* (John Day Co., 1934), p. 132.

10. Edmund A. Moore, *A Catholic Runs for President* (New York: The Ronald Press Co., 1956), p. 21.

11. Ibid., p. 41.

12. Ibid., pp. 146, 176.

13. Williams, *Shadow of the Pope*, p. 318.

14. Richard Hofstadter, "Could a Protestant Have Beaten Hoover in 1928?" *Reporter*, 17 March 1960.

15. David Burner, *The Politics of Provincialism: The Democratic Party in Transition, 1918-1932* (New York: Alfred A. Knopf, Inc., 1968), p. 208-209.

16. Eleanor Roosevelt, *The Autobiography of Eleanor Roosevelt* (New York: Harper & Row, 1961), p. 148.

17. George Q. Flynn, *Roosevelt and Romanism: Catholics and American Diplomacy* (Westport, CT: Greenwood Press, 1976), p. 112.

19. Ibid., pp. 98-136.

20. Ira V. Birdwhistell, "Southern Baptist Perceptions of and Responses to Roman Catholicism, 1917-1972" (Ph. D. diss., Southern Baptist Theological Seminary, 1975), pp. 74-81.

21. *Jim Farley's Story* (New York, 1948).

22. James F. Byrnes, *All in One Lifetime* (New York, 1958), pp. 118-120.

23. John Cogley, *Catholic America* (New York: Dial Press, 1973), pp. 186-187, 188.

24. Editorial, *Christian Index*, 17 April 1947.

25. Jacob S. Payton, "The Church in Congress," *The Christian Advocate*, 15 April 1948.

26. *Social Questions Bulletin*, Methodist Federation for Social Action, March 1947.

27. F. William O'Brien, "General Clark's Nomination as Ambassador to the Vatican: American Reaction," *Catholic Historical Review*, January 1959.

28. Actually written by Theodore Sorensen.

29. "Both Sides of the 'Catholic Issue,'" *U.S. News & World Report,* 26 September 1960.

Chapter 2
THE CAMPAIGN FOR
THE WHITE HOUSE

Senator John F. Kennedy decided to seek the Presidency at least by 1959. His landslide reelection to the Senate and his expanding record as a spokesman for liberal, progressive causes made him a strong possibility. He was quite different from Al Smith in almost every respect. He had been schooled almost exclusively in non-Catholic private schools. He was a Harvard University graduate and an avid student of history. His *Profiles in Courage*, a biographical study of political integrity, won a Pulitzer Prize. He was literate, urbane, and eloquent.

His legislative record was that of a moderate liberal and he had taken some bold positions on federal aid to education and the independence of Algeria. He understood the important role thrust upon the United States in the international arena and knew instinctively that democracy and liberty had to be made a reality at home before they could be exported.

Kennedy hoped that there would not be a substantial religious question in the 1960 campaign but he soon became aware of the intensity of the issue, even in the quiescent preelection year of 1959. In a *Look* interview (March 3, 1959) Kennedy pledged unequivocal support for the uniquely American principle of church-state separation, opposed public aid for parochial schools, and opposed an ambassador to the Vatican. Most secular journalists and prag-

matic politicians applauded the young senator, but, ironically, many Catholics and some moderate Protestants criticized him for sounding too secular. Kennedy had said, "Whatever one's religion in his private life may be, for the officeholder, nothing takes precedence over his oath to uphold the Constitution and all its parts—including the First Amendment and the strict separation of church and state." Patricia Barrett commented, "Some commentators thought Mr. Kennedy had gone too far in asserting the primacy of political over other loyalties and had thus deepened the cleavage between religion and public life."[1] *America,* the distinguished Jesuit weekly, rebuked him (as they were to do again in early 1962): "Our own reaction to the controverted *Look* interview is one of impatience at the earnest Massachusetts Senator's efforts to appease bigots, rather than of disagreement with the positive points he made. A Catholic political candidate, if he must make a profession of his faith, should not seem to give quarter to religious bigotry, even at the risk of having his words distorted. We were somewhat taken aback, for instance, by the unvarnished statement that 'whatever one's religion in his private life ... nothing takes precedence over his oath ....' Mr. Kennedy doesn't really believe that. No religious man, be he Catholic, Protestant or Jew, holds such an opinion."[2]

Lutheran scholar Martin Marty thought that Kennedy was "spiritually rootless and politically almost disturbingly secular." Robert McAfee Brown, a Presbyterian, thought that in Kennedy's " 'effort' to assure his possible constituency that he is just a regular American, he has succeeded only in demonstrating that he is a rather irregular Christian."[3]

Kennedy's forthright advocacy did not convince the inconvincible. *Religious News Service* reported in November 1959 that the Texas Baptist Convention, "adopted a resolution cautioning members ... against voting for a Roman Catholic candidate," and Alabama Baptists "went on record as protesting against the election of any Roman Catholic as U.S. President." The National Association of Evangelicals adopted a statement that read in part, "Any country the Roman Catholic Church dominates suppresses the right of Evangelicals .... For that reason, thinking Americans view with alarm the possible election of a Roman Catholic as President of the United States."[4]

Typical of hostile comments even before Kennedy was nominated was *Christianity Today*'s assertion that "Protestant voters not at all irrationally would prefer to keep the White House out of the hands of someone who confesses to a foreign earthly power." The Alabama Methodist *Christian Advocate* in June 1959 blasted the state's Methodist governor John Patterson for supporting JFK. It said: "The people of Alabama do not intend to jeopardize their democratic liberties by opening the doors of the White House to the political machinations of a determined power-hungry Romanist hierarchy." For a state that treated blacks as badly as Alabama in the 1950s, the reference to "democratic liberties" is curious, if not amusing.

Dr. Ramsey Pollard, president of the Southern Baptist Convention, announced that he would not "stand by and keep my mouth shut when a man under control of the Roman Catholic Church runs for the Presidency of the United States."[5] Pollard was to open his mouth many times in 1960, mostly to put his foot in it. During the campaign he reportedly told one audience, "My church has enough members to beat Kennedy if they all vote like I tell them to."[6]

Senator Kennedy did well in the early primaries and won convincingly in Wisconsin, where a heavy Catholic Republican crossover contributed to his victory over Senator Hubert Humphrey of Minnesota. The voting results showed a Protestant/Catholic division that would make the religious issue even more crucial. Kennedy had to win the primary on May 10 in heavily Protestant West Virginia if his credibility as a winner was to be established. He won a decisive 62 percent landslide, forcing Humphrey's withdrawal. The last real barrier to the nomination had been met.

Before the West Virginia primary Kennedy addressed the American Society of Newspaper Editors in Washington on April 21, 1960. He told the four hundred newsmen, "I want no votes solely on account of my religion." He warned them not to "magnify" or "oversimplify" the religious issue. "I am not the Catholic candidate for President. I do not speak for the Catholic Church on issues of public policy—and no one in that Church speaks for me." He concluded: "If there is bigotry in the country so great as to prevent fair consideration of a Catholic who has made clear his complete independence and dedication to the separation of church and state, then we ought to know it. But I do not believe this is the case. I

believe the American people are more concerned with a man's views and abilities than with the church to which he belongs. I believe that the founding fathers meant it when they provided in the Constitution that there should be no religious test for office."[7]

Many Protestant leaders endorsed Kennedy's views and commended him publicly. Included were Methodist Bishop G. Bromley Oxnam, Presbyterian Moderator Eugene Carson Blake, Dean Francis B. Sayre of Washington Cathedral, and Dr. Edward Hughes Pruden of Washington's First Baptist Church. Several Methodist, Presbyterian, and Lutheran conclaves rejected resolutions urging defeat of a Catholic candidate.

As Senator Kennedy was being nominated on the first ballot in Los Angeles in July, two significant statements of prominent religious leaders suggested the tenor of the fall campaign. On July 3, Dr. W. A. Criswell delivered a fiery sermon in Dallas's First Baptist Church denouncing "Roman Catholicism's bloody hand" and warning that Kennedy's election would "spell the death of a free church in a free state and our hopes of continuance of full religious liberty in America."[8] Archbishop Karl J. Alter of Cincinnati issued a statement denying that Catholics in America "will use religious toleration here to gain the ascendancy" or "to deprive our fellow citizens of freedom of religion or conscience .... We seek no privileged status; we proclaim our full adherence to the provisions of the Constitution as of now as well as for the future."[9] (Unfortunately for Kennedy, the Vatican newspaper *L'Osservatore Romano* in mid-May declared that the Roman Catholic hierarchy had "the right and duty" to advise Roman Catholics how to vote. This editorial was designed for Italy but its timing and tastelessness hurt Kennedy's chances.)

The religious issue smoldered in late summer and started burning by September. Bruce Felknor of the FCPC warned on August 25 that "the circulation of rabidly anti-Catholic material" led to "a substantial danger that the campaign will be dirtier on the religious issue than it was in 1928."[10]

On September 7 at Washington's fashionable Mayflower Hotel, 150 conservative, evangelical, and fundamentalist Protestants of 37 denominations held a one-day national conference of the so-called Citizens for Religious Freedom. Such notables as Dr. Norman

Vincent Peale, of *The Power of Positive Thinking* fame, Dr. Daniel A. Poling, editor of *Christian Herald*, Dr. L. Nelson Bell of *Christianity Today*, and Dr. Harold J. Ockenga, author and theologian, appeared. The group issued a policy statement, denying that it was bigotry to question the credentials of a Roman Catholic candidate. They felt that "it is inconceivable that a Roman Catholic president would not be under extreme pressure by the hierarchy of his church to accede to its policies." The statement drew attention to religious liberty problems in many Catholic countries and alleged canon law restrictions on a Catholic President's attendance at interfaith worship services. It pointed out that Kennedy had favored public aid to parochial schools while in the 81st Congress, though admitting that he was the only Roman Catholic senator to oppose the Morse Amendment, which would have provided partial grants and loans for parochial school construction. They claimed that "the nature of the Roman Catholic Church" created "the religious issue in the present campaign."[11]

On the face of it there were several absurdities, non sequiturs, and downright faulty reasoning in this group's statement. They denounced religious persecution in Catholic countries, as if Senator Kennedy should be blamed for these excesses. Why not blame Protestant candidates for anti-Catholic discrimination in Sweden? They drew attention to Ohio, "a state with a Roman Catholic governor," where "nuns may be placed on the public payroll as school teachers according to an attorney general's ruling."

They failed, conveniently, to mention that the Ohio attorney general was a Protestant and that these conditions had occurred under several Protestant governors. This was rank dishonesty.

The statement was immediately denounced by Dr. Harold E. Fey, editor of the *Christian Century* (September 14, 1960), and a critic of Catholicism himself. "It misrepresents the breadth of Protestant interests, the intelligence of Protestant concerns, the charity of Protestant attitudes." Scholars Reinhold Niebuhr and John C. Bennett called it "blind prejudice," and then noted significantly, "Most of those Protestants who have been in the forefront of this effort would oppose any liberal Democrat regardless of his religion."[12] The Niebuhr-Bennett statement has great import. Without question, the Citizens for Religious Freedom were prepon-

derantly Republican and conservative. They had a streak of cultural snobbery, a belief that only WASPs were good Americans, that a Catholic or a Jew or a slightly offbeat Protestant should not be President. Dr. Peale expressed that view beautifully when he said: "Our American culture is at stake .... I don't say it won't survive, but it won't be what it was."[13] Someone should have told the good doctor that America had long since entered a post-Protestant phase, perhaps even a post-Christian one. (Adlai Stevenson is supposed to have quipped in Minneapolis, "I find St. Paul appealing and St. Peale appalling.") Peale was apparently embarrassed by the publicity surrounding his participation in the conference and he later disassociated himself from it.

It was apparent to Senator Kennedy and his staff that he had to make a dramatic declaration of independence from his church's political involvement in order to allay the lingering suspicions of many Protestants. He accepted an invitation to address the Ministerial Association of Greater Houston on September 12, 1960. Before perhaps a thousand ministers and laymen, and thousands more who would watch the event on television, Kennedy directly confronted the issue and pledged absolute adherence to the U.S. Constitution. He promised to resign rather than submit to clerical dictation. In words that will echo through the centuries, he said: "I believe in an America where the separation of church and state is absolute—where no Catholic prelate would tell the President (should he be Catholic) how to act and no Protestant minister would tell his parishioners for whom to vote—where no church or church school is granted any public funds or political preference—and where no man is denied public office merely because his religion differs from the President who might appoint him or the people who might elect him.

"I believe in an America that is officially neither Catholic, Protestant nor Jewish—where no public official either requests or accepts instructions on public policy from the Pope, the National Council of Churches, or any other ecclesiastical source—where no religious body seeks to impose its will directly or indirectly upon the general populace or the public acts of its officials—and where religious liberty is so indivisible that an act against one church is treated as an act against all."

He reminded the listeners that prejudice against one faith should be construed as prejudice against all. "For while this year it may be a Catholic against whom the finger of suspicion is pointed, in other years it has been, and may someday be again, a Jew—or a Quaker—or a Unitarian—or a Baptist." Almost emotionally and poignantly he reminded fair-minded Americans that thousands of Catholics and Jews died fighting for the freedom we all enjoy today.

"This is the kind of America I believe in—and this is the kind of America I fought for in the South Pacific and the kind my brother died for in Europe. No one suggested then that we might have a 'divided loyalty,' that we did 'not believe in liberty' or that we belonged to a disloyal group that threatened 'the freedom for which our forefathers died.'

"And in fact this is the kind of America for which our forefathers did die when they fled here to escape religious test oaths, that denied office to members of less favored churches, when they fought for the Constitution, the Bill of Rights, the Virginia Statute of Religious Freedom, and when they fought at the shrine I visited today—the Alamo. For side by side with Bowie and Crockett died Fuentes and McCafferty and Baily and Badillo and Carey—but no one knows whether they were Catholics or not. For there was no religious test there."[14]

To thunderous applause Kennedy exited from the room. The conference was televised again and again during the remaining weeks of the campaign.

Kennedy was reinforced by two important declarations. On September 12 one hundred Protestant, Catholic, Jewish, and Greek Orthodox churchmen and scholars issued a statement deploring the religious issue as a violation of Article VI of the U.S. Constitution that "no religious test shall ever be required as a qualification to any office or public trust under the United States." It denounced "the exclusion of members of any family of faith from public office on the basis or religious affiliation." Episcopal bishops were prominently identified with this declaration. The Presiding Bishop, Right Reverend Arthur C. Lichtenberger, Bishops Horace Donegan of New York, Angus Dun of Washington Cathedral, James Pike of San Francisco, Henry Knox Sherrill, and Dean Francis B.

Sayre of Washington Cathedral were among the signers. Methodist Bishop G. Bromley Oxnam, Baptist Dr. Carlyle Marney, and Methodist Dr. Dudley Ward were included. The group listed ten principles as "guidelines for action in the 1960 election." They are:

1. The exclusion of members of any family of faith from public office on the bases of religious affiliation violates the fundamental conditions of a free democratic society, as expressed in the spirit and letter of our Constitution.

2. The religious faith of a public officer is relevant to the conduct of his office .... Inquiry regarding this relevancy is an exercise of responsible citizenship, if conducted in such a way as not to violate the constitutional prohibition against any religious test for public office.

3. No citizen in public office dares to falsify either to his conscience or to his oath of office ... if he cannot reconcile the responsibilities entailed by his oath with his conscience, then he must resign.

4. The fact that a major religious group has so far never furnished the Nation with a candidate who won election to a particular office does not obligate the voters to elect a candidate of that faith to that office sorely to demonstrate our devotion to democracy.

5. No religious organization should seek to influence and dominate public officials for its own institutional advantage.

6. Every person of every faith must be accorded full religious liberty, and no person should be coerced into accepting any religious belief or practice.

7. A candidate's faith, and his affirmations of it, as they bear upon his responsibilities in public office, should be viewed in their best light rather than their worst.

8. The public officer after his election is obligated to make his appointments to subordinate positions on a non-discriminatory basis using competence and record rather than religious affiliation as the criteria of selection.

9. If for reasons of his own he [the President] feels that participation in a particular religious ceremony is not in order, it would be contrary to the civic character of American presidency for him to feel obligated to accept the invitation.

10. He (the President) will recognize that the values in historic faiths other than his own must be brought to bear upon his problems of the day.[15]

On October 5, "A Statement on Religious Liberty by American Catholic Laymen," signed by 166 prominent Catholics from every walk of life, was published. It was the clearest defense of religious

freedom and separation of church and state ever issued by an American Catholic group. It was widely and deservedly praised.[16]

Other groups seeking to counter the continuing viciousness of religious slander included the American Jewish Committee; the American Jewish Congress; the National Council of Churches; the Anti-Defamation League of B'nai B'rith, which exposed the hate literature; the previously mentioned Fair Campaign Practices Committee; and the National Conference of Christians and Jews.

Unfortunately, and not unexpectedly, the unappeasable bigots made a major effort in the campaign's home stretch to defame Kennedy and his faith. Author James Michener, who played a leading role in the Kennedy campaign in Bucks County, Pennsylvania, was sickened and shocked by the flood of anti-Catholic literature spreading throughout his well-educated and presumably enlightened county. Lurid photos of Protestants being burned and tortured by leering priests filled the mailboxes of residents. One Lutheran minister reportedly warned his congregation that Protestants would be hanged in the town square of Levittown if Kennedy were elected. Michener feared the impact of such irrationality and thought Kennedy might lose the election because of it.[17]

It should be noted in passing that America's intellectual community strongly favored Kennedy. He received the endorsements of most of the significant journals of opinion: *Harper's, Atlantic, New Republic, New Leader, Nation, Progressive,* etc. Most intellectuals likely shared the judgment of Arthur Schlesinger that Richard Nixon was the "hollow man" of American politics, without principle, substance, or vision. Although their hearts belonged to Adlai Stevenson, they agreed with Stevenson that Nixon was a middle-class Joe McCarthy, dangerously unfit to lead America through the uncertain 1960s. (To his credit, Nixon denounced the use of religion in the campaign, though he did seem to say in one of the Kennedy-Nixon debates that no atheist could ever be considered a potential President.)

Dulce and Richter noted that "the religious issue had 'gone underground' following the repercussions of the Peale controversy and the Houston speech, but it continued to add no less heat to the steadily intensified campaign."[18] Conservative Protestants attempted to make Reformation Sunday, October 30, an occasion for

a last-ditch "stop Kennedy" effort. Some Catholic bishops in Puerto Rico at this time called on Catholic voters to oust Governor Munoz Marin, who supported divorce and birth control. Some Protestants seized on this local hierarchy's decision as "proof" that Kennedy could not disentangle himself from his bishops. Some of the attacks on Kennedy were absurd as well as unfair. One Baptist preacher in St. Louis formed an "unlock" club. His supporters wore buttons showing Baptist churches in Spain padlocked, and said that they would vote against Kennedy unless and until Baptist churches in Spain were reopened.

Eight state Baptist conventions adopted anti-Kennedy resolutions as did the Assemblies of God, the American Baptist Association, the Augustana Lutheran Church, and the Conservative Baptist Association of America. Most Protestant journals, notably excepting Episcopalians, expressed fear or hesitancy even after Kennedy's declaration of intent.[19] Many Baptist pastors in Texas, North Carolina, Arkansas, and elsewhere worked openly in Nixon's campaign and raised the religious issue.[20]

Still, some Baptists applauded Kennedy. Former President Harry Truman campaigned hard for JFK in the South, and, by his own admission, "cussed out the Baptists," and brought vivid denunciation upon himself by many Baptist preachers. Walter Pope Binns, president of William Jewell College in Missouri, endorsed Kennedy and was given credit by Truman for JFK's razor-thin edge in that state.[21] Several prominent Baptist pastors (especially those who served university congregations) denounced religious bigotry, including Washington's Edward Pruden, who later reflected on JFK's Houston address:

I think I have never heard a finer delineation of our American heritage in this area of our common life. I jokingly accused one of our Baptist experts on the subject of having written the speech for Mr. Kennedy .... In view of the candidate's forthrightness and his disarming expressions of personal convictions regarding basic issues, I felt that it was unfair and un-American to suggest that he should not be considered for the Presidency because of his Catholic affiliation .... I thought it wrong to suggest that any American should be barred from any public office because of his religion.[22]

E. S. James, editor of the Texas *Baptist Standard* was so impressed by JFK and disillusioned by Nixon's equivocation on and Lodge's open support for parochiaid that he strongly implied support for JFK in his final pre-election editorial.[23]

Both political and religious leaders expressed relief as the nasty campaign ended. The FCPC, in a report issued in 1962, analyzed 1,383 reports of 402 "unfair" anti-Catholic political attacks and 392 pieces of "unfair" anti-Catholic literature. The largest numbers were distributed in California, Pennsylvania, and Minnesota, and the committee estimated that 20 to 25 million pieces of such literature were circulated in the United States. The literature was placed in four categories: vile, 5 percent; dishonest, 25 percent; unfair, 35 percent; and responsible, 35 percent. Patricia Barrett has written, "Although the volume of printed matter dealing with the religious issue in the 1960 campaign was *substantially* greater [author's emphasis] than in 1928, the quality was, on the whole, higher."[24]

The *Journalism Quarterly* discovered in a survey of Southern Baptist religious journals that anti-Catholicism was even more pervasive in 1960 than it had been in 1928.[25]

In a tense, dramatic election, with a record turnout of 68.3 million voters, John F. Kennedy was narrowly elected. Religion was a major factor in the structure of the vote and, on balance, Kennedy lost more than he gained because of it. Though most of the religious issue was disgraceful, there was a silver lining that Dulce and Richter observed: "The election of a President of Catholic faith in 1960 gave a ringing stamp of recognition to pluralism as an indelible fact of national and political and social life .... The religious issue generated healthy discussion regarding the separation of church and state, and also raised questions as to the proper degree and the character of influence exercised by churches in the country's political affairs."[26]

A strong majority of Jews (82 percent), Catholics (78 percent), and blacks (75 percent) voted for JFK, as did 38 percent of Protestants. On balance, according to a University of Michigan Survey Research Center survey, he lost 1.5 million net votes because of

religion. JFK's dramatic handling of the religious issue and his sensitivity to Protestant concerns saved the day.

It is obvious that JFK would not have won the 1960 elections without convincing a substantial number of Protestant and non-affiliated voters that he would resist clerical pressures in the exercise of his office. He also had to convince voters of all faiths that he was capable and competent and that his programs would be beneficial to the nation. He won 38 percent of the Protestant vote, as we have seen—barely enough to squeak by Nixon. Yet, he won more Protestant votes (18 million) than Catholic (13.3 million) or Jewish (2.7 million) votes combined.

Other factors emerged as significant. The increase in the Catholic population to 22 percent of the total was important, as was its strategic geographical location in reference to the electoral college. Since many conservative Protestants avoid politics as worldly and sinful, and since millions of black Protestants were not allowed to vote in the South, the Catholic percentage of the total vote was at least 25 percent. Though JFK's 78 percent Catholic vote was lower than Smith's percentage in 1928, he won just enough Catholic support in crucial areas to win. His Jewish and black support were also mightily important in critical states.

The increase in tolerance and the impact of some early ecumenical encounters were also factors. The percentage of voters explicitly opposed to any Catholic President had declined to 20 percent from 30 percent two decades earlier. This hard-core bigot vote was still frighteningly high, and resulted in some very close results and unexpected defeats in certain areas. Still, JFK probably could not have won in 1950 or earlier, due to a great militance and solidarity among non-Catholic voters.

Donald C. Lord discovered that Kennedy's candidacy also caused problems for his supporters in mostly Protestant congressional districts. "Tragically, the young president's election was probably responsible for the defeat of twenty-two Northern Democrats who supported his campaign pledges. Most of these defeated candidates lived in predominantly Northern Protestant areas that usually elected Democratic congressmen in close elections. But a Catholic presidential candidate on the ticket meant defeat for these Northern liberals who supported his programs."[27]

Most religious figures accepted the outcome, but a few gave vent to sour paranoia. "Southern Baptists lost the election. The Roman hierarchy has their man in the White House," lamented the Kansas Baptist weekly.[28] A Kentucky editor was incensed that so many Kentucky Baptists had voted for JFK.[29] In November the *Baptist Standard* published two articles warning of the imminent danger to liberty in JFK's victory, but its editor E. S. James predicted, "We may experience the most definite separation of church and state during the next four years that this century has known." This prophetic observation brings us to the threshold of JFK's Presidency, where we shall see how the prediction came to pass.

Notes

1. Patricia Barrett, *Religious Liberty and the American Presidency* (Herder & Herder, Inc., 1963), p. 9.

2. "On Questioning Catholic Candidates," *America*, 7 March 1959.

3. Robert McAfee Brown, "Senator Kennedy's Statement," *Christianity and Crisis*, 16 March 1959.

4. *New York Times*, 11 April 1959.

5. *New York Times*, 11 February 1960.

6. Theodore Sorensen, *Kennedy* (New York: Harper & Row, 1965), p. 194.

7. *U.S. News & World Report*, 2 May 1960.

8. *New York Herald Tribune*, 5 July 1960.

9. Karl J. Alter, "A Catholic President," *Sign*, July 1960.

10. *New York Times*, 2 August 1960.

11. Barrett, *Religious Liberty and American Presidency*, pp. 149-152.

12. *New York Herald Tribune*, 11 September 1960.

13. *Newsday*, 8 September 1960.

14. Barrett, *Religious Liberty and American Presidency*, pp. 160-164.

15. Ibid., pp. 152-160.

16. Ibid., pp. 164-166.

17. James A. Michener, *Report of the County Chairman* (New York: Random House, Inc., 1961).

18. Berton Dulce and Edward J. Richter, *Religion and the Presidency* (New York: Macmillan Company, 1962), p. 196.

19. Eugene Bianchi, *John XXIII AND American Protestants* (Corpus Books, 1968), pp. 95-112.

20. Ira V. Birdwhistell, "Southern Baptist Perceptions of and Responses to Roman Catholicism, 1917-1972" (Ph. D. Diss., Southern Baptist Theological Seminary, 1975), pp. 97-115.

21. Harry S. Truman to Walter Pope Binns, 21 November 1960.

22. Edward Hughes Pruden, *A Window on Washington* (New York: Vantage Press, 1976), pp. 116-117.

23. E. S. James, "Vote Your Convictions," *Baptist Standard*, 2 November 1960.

24. Barrett, *Religious Liberty and American Presidency*, p. 29.

25. "Change in Attitudes Toward a Catholic for President," *Journalism Quarterly*, Winter 1963.

26. Dulce and Richter, *Religion and the Presidency*, pp. 216-217.

27. Donald C. Lord, *John F. Kennedy* (Woodbury, NY: Barron, 1977), pp. 94-95.

28. *Baptist Digest*, 26 November 1960.

29. "After the Election," *Western Recorder*, 17 November 1960.

Chapter 3
CHURCH, STATE, AND THE KENNEDY PRESIDENCY

John F. Kennedy had given such explicit guarantees about his commitment to religious liberty that discerning observers believed the Kennedy Presidency might be relatively free of religious rancor. JFK had, in fact, restated his belief in a religiously neutral, secular state on CBS's "Face The Nation" on Reformation Sunday: "We do not want an official state church. If ninety-nine percent of the population were Catholics, I would still be opposed to it. I do not want civil power combined with religious power .... I want to make it clear that I am committed *as a matter of deep personal conviction* to separation. Now, what is there left to say?" [Author's emphasis.]

Nevertheless, many conservative Protestants were still suspicious and wary about the Kennedy Presidency. Some self-appointed watchdogs promised to wait and see if the President "so much as raised his little finger" in support of the Roman hierarchy. They had little reason to worry about the President. It was most of the hierarchy, however, that misinterpreted Kennedy's declarations and insisted on pressing the issue of parochial school aid even before JFK had time to try out the White House furniture.

If there was any one domestic issue about which Kennedy felt strongly, it was education. "He devoted more time ... to this single topic than to any other domestic issue."[1] Kennedy believed

that the federal government had a legitimate need and an awesome historic responsibility to improve public education at every level and to make it possible for every deserving child to obtain as much education as possible. He tried for an omnibus bill for education, but when it was blocked by standpatters in Congress, he sought categorical grants for specific programs. He sought to extend the National Defense Education Act of 1958 and to aid universities in the Higher Education Facilities Act of 1963.

Kennedy also favored aid to teachers' salaries, classroom construction, expanded library facilities, new vocational-technical centers, federally approved or guaranteed scholarship loans for needy students, literacy programs, aid to retarded and handicapped children, school lunch and library programs, and educational television. The Office of Education called the Kennedy legislative proposals the most far-reaching in a century.

There was a fly in the ointment, however. Roman Catholic lobbyists, primarily in the National Catholic Welfare Conference (NCWC)—now the U.S. Catholic Conference—demanded that parochial schools be included in all federal programs. This had been a long-standing NCWC policy position and they saw no reason to alter it because a Catholic was now President. Southern conservatives and segregationists, who feared federal pressure for civil rights and equal educational opportunities for blacks, and Republican conservatives, who opposed all federal aid to education on ideological grounds, allied themselves with the NCWC. Even before Inauguration Day, Cardinal Spellman, the semi-official U.S. primate, blasted the Kennedy task force report on education as "unthinkable" for not including parochial schools. The President was outraged at Spellman's intransigence and told Ted Sorensen, "He never said a word about any of Eisenhower's bills for public schools only, and he didn't go that far in 1949 either."[2]

JFK refused to budge. He presented his program in Congress and excluded sectarian schools "in accordance with the clear prohibition of the Constitution." The NCWC immediately called for the defeat of all federal aid to education unless loans to parochial schools were included. JFK tartly commented at a press conference a few days later: "The Catholic, Protestant, and Jewish clergy are entitled to their views, but they should not change their views

merely because of the religion of the occupant of the White House.''³

A comprehensive legal brief prepared by both the Departments of Justice and Health, Education, and Welfare defended the Kennedy proposal and warned against any breach in the wall of separation. The brief did conclude, however, that private and church-related colleges might receive some indirect, peripheral public aid because their nature and curricula were structured to prevent some of the constitutional problems. The brief also allowed busing, school lunches, and secular textbooks for parochial schools under the NDEA's limited aid program. All other forms of public assistance were verboten by the First Amendment.

Kennedy remained incensed when Cardinal Spellman claimed that passage of the Kennedy bill would mean the end of parochial schools in the United States. His Eminence seemed to have forgotten that parochial schools were doing well in 1961, were continuing to attract almost half of the Catholic school-age children without public support (which in itself is insignificant, since canon law demanded that all Catholic children attend church schools). For generations poor Catholic immigrants had provided for their own schools and had not sought public funds. Many Catholic laymen, both liberal and conservative, opposed public aid.

The Kennedy bill passed the Senate, but the real battle was destined to be the House. The parochiaid lobby's auxiliary arm, Citizens for Educational Freedom (CEF), called for a nationwide campaign to block the Kennedy bill and threatened to defeat any congressperson opposed to aiding church schools. The anti-parochiaid forces led by Protestants and Other Americans United for Separation of Church and State (POAU)—now Americans United—and the NEA also moved their campaign into high gear. *Church & State*, POAU's monthly journal, was amazingly sanguine in its February 1961 issue: "We believe that the new President is a man of honor and that he will keep his pledges."

Church and State was also delighted that Kennedy's cabinet was religiously well balanced: two Jews, Presbyterians, and Methodists, and one Mormon, Catholic, Lutheran, and Episcopalian.

Christian Century (January 4, 1961) also editorially commended the President's "mature disregard of religious affiliation" in his

cabinet selections. "The fact that only one Roman Catholic was appointed to the cabinet should go far toward alleviating the fears of some Protestants that a Roman Catholic in the office of chief executive would saturate the government with members of his own faith."

Cardinal Spellman pounded the pavements, contending that Kennedy's proposal "discriminates against Catholics who choose a God-centered education"; was an effort "to use economic compulsion to force parents to relinquish their rights to have religion taught to their children"; and constituted a deprivation of "freedom of religion." Most Protestant and Jewish leaders roundly denounced Spellman and urged acceptance of the Kennedy plan to aid the starved, underfunded public schools. Five national Jewish organizations issued a joint statement, saying, in part, "We deem the maintenance and furtherance of the Jewish religion to be the responsibility of the Jewish community, a responsibility which we have no desire to impose upon the American taxpayer."[4]

One needed a scorecard to tell the players in Congress. Senator Joseph Clark (D-Pa.), a Unitarian liberal Democrat and Kennedy supporter, announced that he would introduce the loan amendment that the bishops demanded. Senator Mike Mansfield (D-Mont.), majority leader of the Senate and a Catholic, sided with the President.

Many Catholic congressmen felt torn loyalties in the Kennedy-Spellman clash. Representative John W. McCormack of Massachusetts, Democratic majority leader of the House, supported the bishops and pleaded for long-term low interest loans for construction of nonpublic schools.

Most Catholic journals supported the hierarchy, with the notable exception of *Commonweal*, the voice of progressive, enlightened Catholicism. Cardinal Cushing, always the loyal friend, tried to use his influence to support the President's plan. Cushing had long opposed aid to parochial schools because of his fear of government entanglement and control. Cushing urged Catholics to recognize the strength of opposition to parochiaid and "neither force such legislation through at the expense of national disunity or use their political influence in Congress to block other legislation of benefit to education because they do not get their own way."[5] A very temperate statement from the salty old Boston cardinal.

Commonweal editorialized on July 7, 1961: "We think the administration's general aid to education bill should be passed." It blasted the two Catholic members of the Rules Committee, Delaney and O'Neill, for keeping the bill bottled up in committee. Such an action is "arbitrary, undemocratic ... circumvention of the legislative process." "Not least among the regrettable aspects of the Delaney-O'Neill maneuver is that it may rekindle animosities." *Commonweal* also published a piece by Father George H. Dunne, who contended, "American Catholics should be happy that the President takes the position he does. ... It is surely in the interest of the church in the United States that the first Catholic President prove beyond any shadow of doubt that his political judgments are not subject to dictation by the hierarchy."[6]

America's erstwhile education specialist, Fr. Charles M. Whelan, though defending parochiaid as both constitutional and necessary for educational pluralism and religious liberty, also recognized "another Catholic position" which is "wholly consistent" with the hierarchy's position. "It emphasizes that the church is essentially a religious society and must be willing to suffer temporal injustice rather than be identified simply as one more political pressure group." Whelan goes on to say: "When a particular program threatens to distort the public image of the church, that program calls for special scrutiny. The Catholic appeal for federal aid to church schools, as widely interpreted in the nation today, does distort the public image of the church. We stand accused by men of goodwill of placing our special interests above the general welfare."[7]

Kennedy aide Ralph Dungan, HEW Secretary Abraham Ribicoff, and adviser Theodore Sorensen tried to convince the bishops and their staff that Kennedy's proposals were sound, constitutional, but in no way anti-Catholic. The administration, they contended, had no objections to purely peripheral school lunches, health services, or transportation services being extended to nonpublic school children. But to no avail. If parochial schools were excluded, the bishops said, no aid should go to public schools.

Major Protestant bodies joined the National Education Association and other groups in opposing any inclusion of parochial schools in federal aid programs. Dr. Gerald E. Knoff, an official with the National Council of Churches, testified on March 16, 1961

before the House Subcommittee on Education. His views epitomize the anti-parochiaid position.

> Nothing is more clear than the likelihood that if substantial grants or loans to church related elementary and secondary schools were made possible, many religious denominations would come to the conclusion that they too should step forward to the public treasury and claim what they would consider their share of federal funds.
>
> If this should happen we believe that our American democracy would be impaired by the increasing fragmentation of education with its inevitable result of cultural segregation. Public schools would be undermined and a cultural schism would develop which would tend to impair our democracy.
>
> The denominations of the National Council of Churches do not believe that such a development would be for the good of our beloved America, no matter what church or synagogue our people worship in and no matter what schools their children attend from Monday morning to Friday afternoon."[8]

Christian Century expressed a view common to Protestants of all persuasions. "Charges that the omission of parochial schools from the administration's education bill is a discrimination against Roman Catholics is wholly without foundation. The Roman Catholic hierarchy in its condemnation of the Kennedy bill and in its warning that it will fight any bill which does not include aid to parochial schools is demanding not equality but preference and patronage. Such a claim cannot be granted within the provisions of the Constitution and under the plain restrictions of the First Amendment."[9]

The secular press, including the *New York Times,* the *Washington Post*, the *Washington Star*, and most liberal independent journals supported the Kennedy position. The *U.S. News and World Report* and *Life*, which had supported Nixon in 1960, supported the Catholic hierarchy's position. A Gallup poll in late April found that 57 percent of voters wanted public funds confined to public schools, while 36 percent wanted parochial and private schools included. Protestants were 63 to 29 percent for public school aid only, while Catholics were 66 to 28 percent in favor of parochiaid. On that issue the President's position was clearly the majority one. Once again JFK espoused a position not in favor with the majority of his co-religionists.

Late in July the die was cast. The House Rules Committee, by an eight to seven vote, killed the Kennedy bills and made it impossible for them to be considered again without invoking the rarely used discharge petition or suspension of rules. The key vote was cast by Representative James J. Delaney, a conservative Catholic Democrat from Queens, New York, who is regarded as the closest thing to a "professional" Catholic lobbyist in Congress. (He is immensely popular in his district and receives Republican as well as Democratic votes.) Delaney was regarded as "Spellman's man" and he was widely blamed or praised for the defeat of the entire JFK federal aid package. *Church & State* (September 1961) called the defeat an example of "clerical blackmail."

The complexity of the Rules Committee vote was lost on some. The committee was supposed to consider both Kennedy's omnibus bill for public schools and a bill, which just passed the House Education and Labor Committee, that provided for $375 million in loans through NDEA for nonpublic schools. The loans would be given for the construction of classrooms and laboratory facilities for the teaching of mathematics, foreign languages, and science. The bill was opposed by the NEA and strict separationists. Rep. Delaney, the apparent swing vote, insisted that all bills be rewritten into one measure, in effect making parochiaid part of a package deal. To get aid for public schools, members would have to vote to include parochials. When this move was defeated, Delaney said he wanted "to clear the air" and voted against all aid.

Given the interfaith tensions, it was understandable that Protestants would blame Delaney and by extension the Roman Catholic Church for the defeat. *Christian Century,* in an angry editorial, "Hierarchy Kills School Aid," said: "Federal aid to public education is dead. The hierarchy of the Roman Catholic Church cannot escape—indeed, is probably willing to accept—blame for the death blow to Kennedy's education proposals .... The hierarchy unabashedly put its special pleas ahead of the nation's needs and threatened to pull down the whole house if it could not have its way."[10] It charged that the hierarchy had shown "no catholicity of charity, justice or concern" but rather had engaged in "shortsighted, indulged self-interest." In an accompanying editorial, though, the *Century* hailed the favorable votes of the other two

Catholic congressmen (O'Neill of Massachusetts and Madden of Indiana), saying that they "are to be commended for rising above sectarian interests in their concern for the nation's problems."

Most Protestant and secular journals agreed with the *Century*'s assessment. The Georgia Baptist weekly commented, "We were wrong about President Kennedy, but we were not wrong about the Roman Catholic Church. It is superb in the game of power politics. It demands instead of asking. It doesn't threaten reprisals, it guarantees them."[11]

A battle royal between Oregon's choleric Senator Wayne Morse and Francis Cardinal Spellman added to the August heat. Morse blasted the bishops in an address to the American Federation of Teachers:

I have no intention of compromising the principles of federal aid to education with any pressure group, or private school group in America, who seek to take federal aid to education legislation into the political trading mart .... A third category of opponents of federal aid ... include highly influential churchmen such as Cardinal Spellman (who) look upon the public schools as competitors. They feel that pressures for improvement in teachers' salaries and reduction in pupil-teacher load in the public schools will result in a draining away of their own lay teachers ....

I appreciate the magnitude of the problem with which they are faced, but I say in all sincerity that the adamant opposition of the higher Catholic clergy to an improvement to our public educational system except upon their own terms will lead to most unfortunate results. If they succeed temporarily in blocking the legitimate aims of a majority of our people through pressure tactics, they are sowing a wind of discord which will result in a whirlwind of resentment when the people of the country learn the facts ....

I say again to the Catholic bishops, do not insist adamantly in this matter upon an all-or-nothing-at-all policy, for if you do, the latent religious quarrels of past history will be brought to life again, and the fabric of our civil society will be stretched once more to the breaking point."[12]

Cardinal Spellman retorted:

It is our conviction that the administration's proposal, put into legislative form by Senator Morse, is actually if not intentionally discriminatory,

unwittingly anti-Catholic and indirectly subversive of all private education.[13]

Morse had the last word in a Senate address. "The Cardinal
cannot repeal the First Amendment by seeming to ignore it."

At their November 1961 annual meeting, the bishops reiterated
their all-or-nothing position, and blasted the "discrimination" that
Catholics suffer on the education question. The *New York Times*
(November 18, 1961) called the bishops' statement "wholly mis-
leading" and the *Washington Post* said that "public schools are
open without the slightest discrimination to children of every
creed."

The Apostolic Delegate, Archbishop Egidio Vagnozzi, rather
unwisely waded into the stream of controversy in a November 14
address in Philadelphia. He told a conference of twelve hundred
Catholic laymen to support the bishops against the President
because "the bishops know what they are doing."

President Kennedy became a hero in the eyes of many heretofore
critical Protestants. In May 1961 the Southern Baptist Convention
passed a resolution commending Kennedy "for his insistence that
the Constitution of the United States be followed in the matter of
not giving federal aid to church schools."[14] Dr. W. A. Criswell of
Dallas called upon Baptists "to stand behind President Kennedy
and the Constitution."[15]

Protestants and Other Americans United for Separation of
Church and State associate director C. Stanley Lowell told the
press that "we are extremely well pleased with President Kennedy"
whose "strong stand . . . will reassure and inspire all who believe in
the separation of church and state."[16] *Christianity Today* (February 16, 1962), *Christian Herald* (May 1961), and several Lutheran,
Baptist, Methodist, and United Church of Christ journals hailed
Kennedy's courage and tenacity in the face of strong ecclesiastical
pressure. When his aid bill was again brought before Congress in
1962, it was again rejected by the same coalition. Protestant and
Catholic responses were roughly the same.

President Kennedy felt that Catholics were being unfairly singled
out for blame. After all, two of the three Catholic Democrats on
the Rules Committee voted for his public education bill, while all

Protestant Republicans opposed it. The bill's House sponsor was a Catholic. On one test vote, only 6 of 166 Republicans voted for it, and virtually all Southern segregationists voted against it. "That's who really killed the bill," Kennedy told Sorensen, "just as they've killed it for fifty years, not the Catholics."[17]

Kennedy was livid, though, about Cardinal Spellman's role, regarding it as proof that Spellman was a partisan Republican. After all, had not Spellman met President Eisenhower at the Newark airport and rode with him in a limousine past cheering New York crowds on the day of the first Nixon-Kennedy debates? And had not Spellman and four of the U.S. cardinals, plus nine archbishops and fifty-six bishops, sat on the dais during Ike's address to the Golden Jubilee dinner of the National Conference of Catholic Charities? Eisenhower was, after all, campaigning for his heir-apparent Nixon. This, plus the pro-Nixon enthusiasm at the Alfred E. Smith Memorial Dinner on October 19, 1960, convinced the Kennedy entourage that most of the American hierarchy and the Vatican preferred Nixon's election.

Cardinal Cushing reminisced about those days in a 1964 interview. "Some of the hierarchy of the church, I presume, were not in favor of John F. Kennedy being elected President. Some of them had very strange ideas about the influence the millions of Catholics in the United States might exert on a man who would be the first President of the United States who was a Catholic. ... On the matters of federal aid to Catholic education and related subjects, I think his attitude was correct. Some of the hierarchy, like myself, never enthused about such aid for we presumed it would include some form of federal control. Furthermore, there were serious doubts about the constitutionality of such aid .... The members of the Catholic hierarchy who opposed the election of a Catholic President did so because they wished to be perfectly free in expressing opinions on public affairs and legislation that directly or indirectly referred to the freedom of religion."[18]

In other words, what Cushing seemed to be saying was that if certain members of the hierarchy could not control Kennedy, they would have preferred a more malleable Protestant like Nixon.

Fletcher Knebel wrote at the height of the debate, "Whatever the final outcome of the school-aid fight in America—and it may go on

for years—history will note that the country's first Catholic President fought side by side with Protestant leaders against the clergy of his own church.''[19]

An explosive church-state issue, which occurred midway in the Kennedy Presidency, may reveal JFK's broad tolerance and strict separationist orientation more than any other event. On June 25, 1962 the United States Supreme Court ruled in *Engel* v. *Vitale* that school-sponsored or mandated prayers as part of a regularly scheduled devotional exercise were unconstitutional. Public opinion was, in the main, aggressively hostile. Conservative and evangelical Protestants joined with most Catholics and some Jews in vehemently denouncing the decision. The Supreme Court justices were flayed from pulpits across the nation, in the halls of Congress, and in the religious press. Plans were made for a constitutional amendment to overrule the Court. Both Cardinal Spellman and Billy Graham delivered well-published jeremiads against the Court.

America had a black-bordered cover in its July 7, 1962 issue and called its lead editorial "Black Monday Decision." It said, in part: "In this case and its decision, the secularizing tendencies at work in American society have come full circle .... It is quite literally a stupid decision, a doctrinaire decision, an unrealistic decision, a decision that spits in the face of our history, our tradition, and our heritage as a religious people."

America also claimed that the decision "is based on the clamorous and constant protestations of a well-organized and litigious minority," and called on parents to continue to support schools "that are free from the enslaving limitations of secularistic dogma."

In contrast to *America*, with which it is often inaccurately coupled, *Commonweal* presented as a feature article in its July 27, 1962 issue a debate between separationist Leo Pfeffer and accommodationist William Ball. Leo Pfeffer wondered: "What is particularly disturbing is that so much of (the strident reaction to the decision) should come from high-placed Catholic sources, for the Catholics in America have themselves been the victim of this same type of defamation." He continued: "Those who are committed to a secular public school system ... owe a great debt of gratitude to

the Catholic Church and the Catholic community. No factor was more important in the secularization of American public education than the loyalty, courage, and perseverance of Catholic parents who ... fought in the courts and forum of public opinion the numerous religious practices that permeated the public schools in the 19th century.'' This was precisely the reaction I initially felt as I observed the varied reactions to the court decision. Catholic children had been beaten in Massachusetts schools for refusing to read the King James Version of the Bible and recite the Protestant version of the Lord's Prayer. A Massachusetts court upheld this outrageous religious repression in the mid-nineteenth century.

Father John Bapst was tarred, feathered, and ridden out of Ellsworth, Maine on a rail in 1843 because he spoke out against similar practices. Catholic churches and homes were burned to the ground in Philadelphia in 1844, partly as a result of this issue. Catholics joined with Jews and freethinkers in a successful suit against religious coercion in Louisiana public schools. The first major victory, in fact, against school-sponsored religion was won in the Illinois Supreme Court in 1910, on a case brought by Catholic parents in Scott County.

"What has happened," Pfeffer asked, "to make the Catholic Church so bitterly condemn today what it so ardently espoused yesterday?" This is a question for religious sociologists, I suppose, but one explanation may be that Catholicism became more assimilated, less tangential to American life by 1962 than it had been a century before. It forgot the bitter persecution of the past and settled down to a cozy relationship with the culture around it. This explanation is not wholly satisfactory, though, since Catholic attitudes on birth control, abortion, and parochial schools were still distinct and differentiated from non-Catholic opinions in 1962. The hostile Catholic reactions may have stemmed from a growing concern with the increasingly secular nature of American society, and a belief that America's moral fiber was being undermined, thus weakening the nation's ability to repel "atheistic communism"— still a bugbear in those Cold War days.

Dorothy Dohen suggested in *Nationalism and American Catholicism* that U.S. Catholics felt it necessary to overcompensate for the frequent charges of "disloyalty," "dual allegiance," and "un-

Americanism" that were hurled at them. They wanted to belong and be accepted so badly that they adopted many of the WASP cultural mores, among which was a vague religiosity in public schools.

A few Protestants joined most Jews and humanists in defense of the Court. Dean M. Kelly of the National Council of Churches supported the ruling because "it protects the religious rights of minorities and guards against the development of public school religion."

Christian Century reminded its readers that "nothing in the June 25 ruling prevents teachers or pupils in the public schools from engaging in prayer. Private prayer, the kind of prayer honored in Scripture and most often practiced by religious people, remains untouched."[20] It chided Spellman and Graham, saying: "Neither the Cardinal nor the evangelist is ready to accept the fact that under our Constitution the government is and must remain secular." The *Century* also solicited support from thirty-one Protestant churchmen representing twelve denominations. They said: "We believe the Court's ruling against officially written and officially prescribed prayers protects the integrity of the religious conscience and the proper function of religious and governmental institutions." POAU predicted that the decision "will loom as a landmark of religious freedom."[21]

Into this tempest stepped the young President. At his press conference he called for respect for the rule of law. "I think that it is important . . . that we support the Supreme Court decisions even when we may not agree with them. In addition, we have in this case a very easy remedy and that is to pray ourselves . . . . We can pray a good deal more at home, we can attend our churches with a good deal more fidelity, and we can make the true meaning of prayer much more important in the lives of all of our children. That power is very much open to us."[22]

This sincere response to a questioner reveals not only Kennedy's admiration of genuine voluntary religious experience, but his fundamental respect for the legal process. It was an act of magnanimity and courage rare for any President and a sharp contrast to the later demagoguery of President Gerald Ford, who denounced the prayer decisions during the 1976 New Hampshire primary. (On

another occasion Ford practically called for Bostonians to disobey the law on school busing.) And it contrasted with attacks on the Court by former Presidents Hoover and Eisenhower. Gallup polls found that less than 20 percent of voters supported the Court and President on this emotional issue.

Another church-state issue was birth and population control. President Eisenhower said publicly that it is "none of our business" to support effective population control programs in the overpopulated Third World nations. (This made Bishop Fulton Sheen so happy that he called Ike the world's greatest statesman, except for General Franco.) JFK, however, was more sensitive to the needs of nations which could not even begin to tackle their economic and social problems until the runaway birthrate was curbed. Thus, under his administration and "with his support, the Federal government quietly but extensively increased its activities in the area of birth and population control—increasing its research grants, supporting an expansion of United Nation efforts and offering to help make more information available to other countries requesting it."[23]

This not only departed from established United States laissez faire practice, but opposed the U.S. Catholic bishops' declaration of Thanksgiving Day, 1959, that birth control programs must be shunned by the government. The Vatican also disapproved.

How did Catholics respond to these initiatives? Those closely allied with the institutional church were somewhat dismayed, but accepted them as political realities. JFK could not have shown the slightest preference toward his co-religionists without endangering his ability to govern effectively as President of all the people.

America recognized this in its January 13, 1962 cover story, "The Church and the President." It called Kennedy "a faithful, practicing" Catholic, but recognized that "as the first American President to profess the Catholic faith, he was, is and will remain a marked man." The editors recognized that Kennedy had to be a very cautious Catholic "in a land largely dominated, in the cultural sense, by a strong residual Protestant tradition." The journal was a bit irked, though, by Kennedy's refusal to pay attention to Catholic clergy. "Mr. Kennedy has not sought out the advice, assistance, companionship and friendship of highly placed Catholic digni-

taries. Catholic prelates and Catholic clergymen pay few if any calls these days at the White House." The editors were also peeved that Paul Blanshard and the Americans United crowd were welcome at the White House.

America was a bit sarcastic that Kennedy and Billy Graham were apparent friends, noting that such a well-publicized entente was "pure 14-karat gold, to be laid away at 5 percent interest till the day of reckoning in 1964." Finally, they said, "We repeat that Catholics in general are not troubled by the fact that the first Catholic President finds it expedient to walk so softly on so many fragile Protestant eggs. But now and again ... this strategy can hobble the President in his pursuit of important national and international objectives." In other words, in dealing with Catholic countries, the President might wish to emphasize his Catholicism. Most of the Catholic popular and diocesan press concurred in this assessment.

One final church-state issue of the Kennedy days occured in August, 1962 when the Agency for International Development (AID) published a "policy determination" allowing U.S. government foreign aid funds to be distributed through religious organizations abroad. Baptist and separationist groups raised serious constitutional objections, and Bill Moyers told Kenneth O'Donnell that "nothing has so stirred up the leaders of the conservative and fundamental religious organizations in the South and Southwest."[24] President Kennedy immediately moved to rescind the AID policy statement, telling the Baptist General Convention in Colorado that AID policies and procedures must conform "with the constitutional principles which you and I support most strongly."[25]

Once again JFK was a hero to Baptists, and the White House was deluged with congratulatory telegrams from Baptist officials. A laudatory editorial in the *Baptist Standard* pleased Bill Moyers who told O'Donnell, "The way you handled the Baptists on the AID religious policy memorandum paid off."[26]

Protestants grew more warmly attached to the President. E. S. James, editor of the influential Texas *Baptist Standard*, met with President Kennedy in February 1963 and expressed great confidence in the Chief Executive. "Our President is a man of faith who is characterized by great intelligence, much ability, strong convictions, and profound courage. ... He is one Roman Catholic who

has proved he could conduct his office without bias."[27] After the assassination James wrote: "President Kennedy was not a Baptist, but it is safe to say that Southern Baptists have had no better friend in the White House. He defended the principle of religious liberty."[28] Brooks Hays, former President of the Southern Baptist Convention and Special Assistant to President Kennedy, commented after the assassination: "His devotion to freedom and to the Biblical idea of universal love linked him to us as well as to his Catholic people."[29] C. R. Daley, a one-time Kennedy critic, said that the President's greatest legacy was his commitment to church-state separation and religious freedom.[30] *Christianity Today* (December 6, 1963) affirmed that "Kennedy had kept his promise to the nation." The *Journal of Church and State* (Winter 1964) hailed his achievements in church-state relations and praised his "unusual intelligence and integrity."

The imprimatur of former Protestant critics was simply astounding. They viewed the Kennedy Presidency as a golden age for the revitalization of the church-state separation principle. Mrs. Eleanor Roosevelt once commented in the late 1940s that the battle for church-state separation might have to be fought all over again. It was, during the Kennedy Presidency, and a clear victory was won by the separationist side. (History tends to repeat itself, though, and the Nixon-Ford years saw a weakening of the separationist cause in the executive branch of the government.)

In retrospect, there was some unintentionally prophetic writing in Protestant journals shortly before (and even during) Kennedy's Presidency. *Christianity Today*, for example, hoped that Kennedy might initiate a movement in his church to repudiate the attitudes which made most Catholics in public life frightening to non-Catholics.[31] The liberal Episcopalian *Churchman* predicted that Kennedy would have great influence on Roman Catholic church-state views.[32] Elson Ruff of *The Lutheran* thought that the time was now ripe for Roman Catholics to grasp a historic opportunity to prove their commitment to religious freedom and tolerance.[33] David O. Moberg, an evangelical, regarded Kennedy's election as a vindication of religious liberty and fair play in America and predicted that Kennedy would foster a new era in Catholic

attitudes and bring about "a modification of Catholic doctrine and practice relevant to freedom of religion."[34]

Kennedy's entente with the Protestant community began early in his administration. Representatives of the Baptist World Alliance "sought a meeting with the President because they are anxious to heal whatever divisions might have arisen during the campaign."[35] JFK met with these Baptists and graciously allied himself with their aspirations. [See appendix.]

A *New York Times* reporter found that the clergy of Houston, who had "subjected JFK to an inquisition that revealed deep suspicion and foreboding" in 1960, were great admirers of the President in 1962. "A fundamental change of feeling about the presence of a Roman Catholic in the White House" was noted.[36]

The Gallup Poll reported on April 6, 1963 that JFK's "sharpest gains since the 1960 vote have come among Protestants." JFK was polling 58 percent of Protestant votes against Nelson Rockefeller, a gain of 20 percent. JFK had picked up only 8 percent among Catholics and 2 percent among Jews. Dean Francis Sayre of Washington Cathedral said it best: "I think the Protestants came to think that he was really their man."[37]

Summary

JFK's overall record on the major church-state issues of parochiaid, prayer in public schools, birth control, and foreign aid was considered excellent by separationists and Protestant, Jewish, and liberal Catholic groups. On peripheral issues his record was also widely praised. He vetoed a censorship bill aimed at the District of Columbia because he felt it would violate the Bill of Rights. He frequently attended interfaith prayer breakfasts, received the Family of Man award from the Protestant Council of New York and the Brotherhood of Man award from the National Conference of Christians and Jews. He appointed no representative to the Vatican. He showed no religious favoritism in presidential appointments. A POAU study showed that 80 percent of the upper echelon federal appointees under Kennedy were Protestant, while 15

percent were Catholic, and 5 percent Jewish. Of the 120 appointees to the federal judiciary, 80 percent were Protestant, 17 percent Catholic, and 3 percent Jewish. If anything, Catholics were somewhat underrepresented since they form 23 percent of the population.

JFK is sometimes criticized by separationists for appointing Byron White to the U.S. Supreme Court, since White usually interprets the Constitution in an accommodationist posture. History shows, though, that justices often differ with the President who appointed them, even on issues of major concern to the President. (The Supreme Court's Nixon appointees, for example, differed from Nixon's predilections on parochiaid and abortion law.)

Kennedy amazed conservative Protestants, disappointed conservative Catholics, and delighted moderates and liberals of all religious traditions in his handling of vexatious church-state disputes during his thousand days.

The significance of the Kennedy Presidency as far as cultural pluralism is concerned is that it reaffirmed and revitalized the pluralist impulse and led to major accommodations between religious groups. JFK was a free man, as his pre-presidential record, his campaign promises, and his Presidency demonstrated. By being free, he freed many Catholics and Protestants from the debilitating recriminations of the past.

The editors of the prestigious *Journal of Church and State* placed Kennedy in historical perspective. "An examination of President Kennedy's positions and pronouncements on church and state indicates that he embraced the tradition of Washington, Jefferson and Madison....Not since James Madison has any American President so definitely expressed his own position on church-state relations in the American schema." The Kennedy legacy will long remain. "The prejudiced predictions of many of America's nativists and spokesmen of religious divisiveness seem delusory and far removed from the present reality of American life."[39]

Notes

1. Theodore Sorensen, *Kennedy* (New York: Harper & Row, 1965), p. 358.

2. Ibid., p. 360.

3. Washington *Post*, 16 March 1961.

4. *Church & State,* March 1961.

5. Sorensen, *Kennedy,* p. 363.

6. *Commonweal,* 2 June 1961, pp. 247-250.

7. Charles M. Whelan, "School Question: Stage Two," *America*, 1 April 1961, pp. 17-19.

8. *Church & State,* May 1961.

9. "Catholics Demand Patronage," *Christian Century*, 22 March 1961, pp. 381-382.

10. "Hierarchy Kills School Aid," *Christian Century*, 2 August 1961, p. 924.

11. "Church Blocks Federal Funds," *Christian Index*, 29 June 1961, p. 6.

12. *Church & State*, October 1961.

13. Ibid..

14. *Annual* of the Sourthern Baptist Convention, 1961, p. 81.

15. Sorensen, *Kennedy*, p. 363.

16. Ibid.

17. Ibid., p. 362.

18. Oral interview with Cardinal Cushing at Kennedy Library.

19. Fletcher Knebel, "The Bishops vs. Kennedy," *Look*, 23 May 9.1961.

20. *Christian Century*, 4 July 1962.

21. *Church & State*, September 1962.

22. Sorensen, *Kennedy*, p. 364.

23. Ibid.

24. Memo of 22 August 1962 in the White House Central Files, Kennedy Library.

25. Letter of President Kennedy, 22 August 1962, Kennedy Library.

26. Memo of 2 October 1962, white House Central Files, Kennedy Library.

27. E. S. James, "Forty Minutes with President Kennedy," *Baptist Standard*, 27 November 1963.

28. *Baptist Standard*, 27 November 1963.

29. *Biblical Recorder*, 14 December 1963.

30. C. R. Daley, "Profile in Courage," *Western Recorder*, 5 December 1963.

31. Editorial, *Christianity Today*, 26 October 1962.

32. *Churchman*, January 1961.

33. *The Lutheran*, 30 November 1960.

34. David O. Moberg, "A Victory for Religious LIberty?" *Eternity*, February 1961.

35. Memo of Bill Moyers to Kenneth O'Donnell, 2 February 1961, Kennedy Library.

36. Homer Bigart, "Ministers' Fears of Kennedy Fade," *New York Yimes*, 12 September 1962.

37. Oral interview with Dean Francis Sayre, Kennedy Library.

38. *Church & State*, June 1962.

39. "The Curch-State Legacy of JFK," *Journal of Church and State* 6, no. 1 (Winter 1964).

Chapter 4
KENNEDY'S RELIGION: PRIVATE NATURE, PUBLIC IMPLICATIONS

Early Upbringing

Kennedy's family, especially his mother, was devoutly Catholic, and maintained close personal contacts with many leaders of the hierarchy. His father had been a generous contributor to Catholic charities. His mother, Rose, attended Mass every morning, a life-long practice, and molded the children's devotional and prayer life. She taught the catechism on Friday afternoons and listened to their prayers at bedtime.

The family patriarch, Joseph Kennedy, insisted that his sons attend non-Catholic schools. JFK, therefore, attended Dexter Academy, a secular private school in Brookline, and later went to Choate, an Episcopal-related prep school in Connecticut. For only one year did he attend a Catholic school, in this case, Canterbury School in Connecticut, an elite lay-run institution that resembled a proper English "public" school. He then attended Harvard University, which, to most Boston Irish, was "the Kremlin on the Charles." Kennedy thus grew up in a milieu where he encountered Protestants, Jews, and others on a regular basis—a factor that helped to shape his lifelong tolerance and respect for other religions.

Kennedy recognized his family influence when he told the Council of Methodist Bishops in 1959, "I am a strong Catholic and I come from a strong Catholic family."[1] What he may have meant by "strong" at that time is puzzling. The evidence strongly belies it.

JFK went through a normal period of adolescent rebelliousness against religion. Joan and Clay Blair claimed in *The Search for JFK* that he "even considered giving up Catholicism," though I find no evidence to substantiate such a drastic step.

One of Kennedy's naval buddies remembered the internal conflicts that the young JFK felt about his religion. John L. Iles, now a salesman in Shreveport, Louisiana, was Kennedy's roommate at the PT training school in Melville, Rhode Island in late 1942. He told the Blairs: "Jack was going through a troubled time with his religion. ... Jack had lost his religion. He said he'd work it out someday. He told me he'd go see Fulton Sheen when he got home."[2]

If Kennedy ever did so, there is no record of it. Records of Kennedy's private correspondence prior to 1947 are unavailable, and Bishop Sheen declined to discuss the matter with me. I suspect that JFK made some sort of intellectual accommodation with his hereditary faith before embarking on his political career. It may have come as a result of his brushes with death, or as a result of his search for the meaning and purpose of life. He may also have concluded that an ex-Catholic simply could not have been elected in Massachusetts.

Disinterest

JFK had no real intellectual interests in religion nor had he ever had much systematic training in theology. (This is hardly unusual in American society. Religion interests only a minority of people in any meaningful, academic sense.) A listing of book titles in JFK's Bowdoin Street library reveals a total absence of religious books, save for a New Testament and a summary of Catholic doctrine.[3]

Kennedy's closest aide, Theodore Sorensen, who shared the triumphs and tragedies of the Kennedy years, wrote about JFK's religion. "Not once in eleven years—despite all our discussions of

church-state affairs—did he ever disclose his personal views on man's relation to God. ... I never heard him pray aloud in the presence of others."[4]

Kennedy regularly attended church and received the sacraments, but did not make a big production out of it. He accepted the religion he had inherited without feeling either superior or inferior about it. He never apologized for his religion nor did he boast about it.

Billy Graham relates that he and JFK discussed the Second Coming of Christ during one of their meetings. Kennedy was amazed at Graham's discussion and questioned whether the Catholic Church held the same belief. This indicates an extraordinary lack of interest in or knowledge of Catholicism on JFK's part, since the Second Advent is integral to Catholic eschatology. It might also indicate that the sermons Kennedy heard during his life, rarely, if ever, dealt with this theme.

Tolerance

JFK was a very tolerant man. "He did not believe that all virtue resided in the Catholic Church," said Ted Sorensen.[5] He respected all religious traditions and felt that truth may be found in all religions. "He was enormously respectful of all religions," says Dean Sayre.[6] Cardinal Cushing related that Kennedy once told him, "We must esteem other religious faiths."[7] Kennedy, to Lawrence Fuchs, "was a symbol of the dynamic impact of the American environment on Catholicism. ... He was the antithesis of the stereotyped, separatist, parochial, anti-intellectual, superstitious, tribalistic, and fatalistic Catholic of Protestant literature and conversation."[8]

Kennedy abhorred religious divisiveness and provincialism. He was "angered by reports of local clerics who were alleged to oppose interfaith activities or public school bond issues."[9] His personal Senatorial and White House staffs were religiously balanced. As Senator, Kennedy's staff contained relatively few Catholics, far fewer than Vice President Nixon's. Nixon sourly remarked in his self-pitying *Six Crises* that he had more Catholics on his staff than

Kennedy, including personal secretary Rose Mary Woods and speechwriter Father John Cronin. Nixon thought this had entitled him to a larger Catholic vote than he received.

Kennedy's White House personal secretary was a Methodist and his closest staff associate, Ted Sorensen, was a Unitarian. His first cabinet included two Jews for the first time in history (Secretary of Labor Arthur Goldberg and Secretary of Health, Education, and Welfare Abraham Ribicoff).

Kennedy had spoken unreservedly in favor of religious tolerance and pluralism during his presidential campaign. His record as president exemplified this trait in many ways. In a September 1963 address to the United Nations, he pointedly made reference to anti-Buddhist repression in Catholic-run South Vietnam. "Human rights are not respected," he said, "when a Buddhist priest is driven from his pagoda, when a synagogue is shut down, or when a Protestant church cannot open a mission." His reference to Protestant difficulties in South America was extraordinary.

At the centennial observances of Boston College, April 20, 1963, Kennedy told the mostly Catholic audience that "we are learning to talk the language of progress and peace across the barriers of sect and creed." Praising Pope John's recent encyclical *Pacem in Terris*, Kennedy observed: "As a Catholic I am proud of it; and as an American I have learned from it." This was one of the rare instances in which the President mentioned his faith publicly. He was especially pleased that the encyclical "shows that on the basis of one great faith and its traditions there can be developed counsel on public affairs that is of value to all men and women of good will." The President was justly proud of Pope John's numinous and advanced document, but even here he reminded his audience that "it closely matches notable expressions of conviction and aspiration from churchmen of other faiths, ... and from outstanding world citizens with no ecclesiastical standing." The president even included the religiously nonaffiliated in this splendid address. Three weeks later, on his triumphal European tour, he told the Irish Parliament: "The supreme reality of our time is our indivisibility as children of God."

JFK's ecumenism is also revealed in his private charity. He donated his entire salary to Protestant, Catholic, Jewish, and non-

sectarian charities, stipulating that his gifts be given without publicity.[10]

The only criticism that has been made of Kennedy's tolerance was the 1950 incident at the Chapel of the Four Chaplains in Philadelphia. Kennedy, then a young Congressman, accepted but later reneged on an invitation to represent Catholics at the dedication of a chapel devoted to the memory of four naval chaplains who gave their lives for their men during an incident in World War II. Kennedy is supposed to have checked with Philadelphia's Cardinal Dougherty, who advised him against appearing on the program. Kennedy complied. Later, he said that, as a public official, he should not represent one faith. This seems to square, of course, with his strong separationist orientation. The Protestant and Jewish representatives at the interfaith service were clergy. Unfortunately, the Catholic diocese, in those very unecumenical times, declined to send a priest as a participant. Kennedy sought to dissuade Cardinal Dougherty's adamant position but was unsuccessful. The main problem was that the memorial was to be located in a Baptist sanctuary. Kennedy's attendance was, as he explained it, "against the precepts of the Catholic Church. Because of this fact, the Archdiocese of Philadelphia was unable to support the drive. Therefore I felt I had no credentials to attend. As a loyal son of the church, I had no other alternative." This was the only example of JFK's bowing to church pressure, and it was undoubtedly the poor state of Protestant-Catholic relations that shaped the outcome of the incident.[11]

Shortly after this unpleasant incident, though, JFK helped to raise funds for the Woodrow Wilson Tomb at Washington's Episcopal Cathedral. Dean Sayre was honored. "I felt that this was an admirable action on his part since he was a member of a different faith."[12]

Though JFK knew that conservative Protestants were the most likely to be hostile to him, he was also perplexed by some liberal reserve. When Protestant liberals and Catholic conservatives attacked his pro-separation interviews in *Look* in 1959, he told Dean Sayre, "I am being attacked on both sides, and yet I always thought of myself as a good Christian."[13]

Lawrence Fuchs said that JFK believed many liberal intellectuals and Stevensonians were "just prejudiced against Catholics." Fuchs, a liberal himself, concurred. "Many of them were. They had a tremendously strong disposition to disbelieve the possibility of a Catholic's being a free, independent, and liberal President."[14]

A letter JFK wrote on July 31, 1957 further reveals an important facet of his mind-set. "I have always been impressed in my study of American history by the fact that this country has been singularly blessed in its ability to take the best of all religions and cultures— not merely tolerating differences but building a new and richer life upon them. I firmly believe that our religious and cultural pluralism has been over the years one of our principal sources of strength."[15]

A Private Matter

Kennedy was certainly not ashamed of his faith. He attended Mass regularly and matter-of-factly during the primary and general election campaigns in heavily Protestant states. He preferred that there be no press attention to what he saw as an intensely private act. He wanted no publicity even on his foreign travels. During his European visit in June 1963, Kennedy attended Mass in the tiny Chapel of Our Lady of the Forest in the charming Sussex village of Forest Row. He refused a front pew or a sanctuary seat. He wanted no photographers or special favors of any kind—just a quiet time to worship in his quiet way.[16]

In politics, too, Kennedy resented being known as a Catholic. When being considered for the Vice Presidency in 1956, Kennedy was somewhat embarrassed by the attention given his religion. On July 31, 1956 he told a reporter that he was not interested in being nominated if his nomination was due solely to his religion. The so-called "Bailey Memorandum" (actually written by Ted Sorensen) had been released to selected press people in an attempt to show that Stevenson needed to attract the pivotal Catholic vote that had defected to Eisenhower in 1952. To do this, it was argued, a Catholic should be on the ticket. The document was valid in a sense, and based on some sound data, but Senator Kennedy soon disavowed it.

Again in 1960 he pleaded that he "was not the Catholic candidate for President but the Democratic candidate who happened to be a Catholic." Kennedy wanted very much to defuse religious antagonism and hence maintained a low religious profile during his public career. "He resented politicians who paraded their religion for political purposes."[17]

Kennedy was not a revanchist. "He had no deep desire to avenge the discrimination his grandparents had encountered in Boston."[18] "And he was not . . . interested in whatever glory attached to being the first Catholic President."[19]

In his Houston address, JFK said, "I believe in a President whose views on religion are his own private affair." He was expressing, so it seems, the traditional American reluctance to regard one's personal religious views as having or being imbued with any public significance. Many theologians would criticize this orientation as one which excessively privatizes religious opinion, but in a nation like the United States, it may also be regarded as a safeguard against constant conflict along religious lines in the political arena.

Brooks Hays relates that JFK "was very sensitive to this matter of religion. He abhorred any parading of piety." He "shied away from overt evidence of religious faith" in "such matters as Church attendance and public prayer." Kennedy had "a desire never to exploit religion, but his utterances all sustain the assurances that he was in the finest sense of the term a devout man."

Hays reveals that JFK was "deeply moved" when told that many Baptists were "constantly praying" for him.[20] Kennedy, in fact, replied to one questioner, "I rely upon God's guidance, and I believe that one of America's greatest strengths is its spiritual faith."[21]

An examination of the White House files indicates that JFK was swamped with personal inquiries about religion. There was much trivia. Some requested that he sponsor their baptism or confirmation, and others offered to send him religious relics or requested his appearance at church events. One Minnesota fundamentalist was angry that Secretary of Agriculture Orville Freeman had given a speech on Sunday evening, thus violating the Sabbath and cutting into the preacher's Sunday night attendance! Other letters asked the President to intercede on behalf of Protestants persecuted in South America.

Many Catholics wrote to inquire if Mass were celebrated at the White House. (It was not.) Some wondered how devout the President was. Inquiries of this nature were answered by Evelyn Lincoln in a form letter response that said, in part: "The President's religious habits are, of course, personal. I can assure you, however, that he is a practicing Roman Catholic. While there is no chapel in the White House, the President and his family are fully able to meet their religious obligations as residents of Washington, D.C. and find it quite convenient to attend Mass."[22] Letters like this do not really add to our knowledge of Kennedy's religion, since they were obviously designed to elicit favorable reactions from the inquirer.

Flexibility

JFK's upbringing and temperament made him an independent-minded Catholic who believed in the autonomy and importance of individual conscience in moral decision making. He accepted some of the premises of situation ethics. He thus approached the more liberal, pragmatic, and flexible ethics that is characteristic of the church today. In the late 1950s he wrote, "There is considerable difference among Catholics with respect to the application of general principles to specific fact situations."[23]

Interest in the Bible

Though it was surprising to many Protestants, John F. Kennedy had a genuine interest in and working knowledge of the Bible. Although he never attended parochial schools or colleges or apparently studied religion in any great depth, he delighted in several Biblical passages and his public addresses were replete with Biblical references. He seemed to prefer the Old Testament, especially the Psalms and Proverbs and the passage from the third chapter of Ecclesiastes, which treats of the changing seasons, the ebb and flow of human life. Courage, integrity, destiny, righteousness, and

dependence on God are the themes that he sought to illuminate in Biblical verse. Tenacity, endurance, and observing one's commitments appear with frequency in the scriptural allusions pervading his speeches.

At the 11th Annual Presidential Prayer Breakfast on February 7, 1963, President Kennedy quoted, as he had many times before, the first verse of the 127th Psalm: "Except the Lord build the house, they labour in vain that build it: except the Lord keep the city, the watchman waketh but in vain." He was planning to quote that passage again at the Trade Mart in Dallas on November 22, 1963.

Kennedy always quoted from the King James Version, revealing his knowledge of it and his appreciation for its matchless literary quality. This would suggest a very "unparochial" approach and an understanding of the Authorized Version's influence on Western culture's literary heritage. Skeptics might charge that his Biblical knowledge does not really prove acceptance of its message on his part, but merely attachment to its literary and oratorical value. Some would suggest that his speechwriters selected verses calculated to impress audiences, but I would tend to give him the benefit of the doubt.

For one thing, Kennedy told West Virginia voters on a Charleston television broadcast on May 8, 1960, that a President would be "committing a sin against God" if he swore falsely on the Bible. Was this campaign hyperbole designed for the Bible-reading voters or was it genuine? I suspect it was the former. On another occasion he told the National Conference of Christians and Jews (November 21, 1961) that "we all draw our guidance, inspiration, and sense of moral direction from...the Bible."

His Baptist advisor Brooks Hays advised him and suggested certain appropriate themes for the Presidential Prayer Breakfasts, so Kennedy's use of the Bible may be partially attributed to this source.[24] Nevertheless, Cardinal Cushing, who knew JFK's religion as well as anyone, said, "He was a great reader of the Bible."[25] Kennedy also gave, as a gift, a Latin Vulgate Bible to the Quayle Bible Collection at Baker University in Baldwin, Kansas in April 1962.

Anticlericalism

The term *anticlerical* is little used in the United States, because clergy have never had the political and social influence here that they have traditionally exercised in other Christian lands. Even within Catholicism, which is most prone to problems of clericalism and anticlericalism, anticlerical outbursts have been relatively rare. However, the American spirit of individualism and independence, the secular nature of the state, and the broad access to education all helped to reduce dependence on a clerical caste.

Kennedy "displayed a remarkably candid irreverence toward ecclesiastical authorities, especially in private,"[26] but his irreverence "did not constitute a rejection of Catholicism."[27] He was known to dislike hypocritical, pompous clerics and he resolutely refused to grant any special political competence to the clergy. "To Kennedy, being a good Catholic did not mean either that he had to be surrounded by Catholics or that he could not sharply disagree with clerical authorities on questions of public policy."[28]

He was quite capable of thinking for himself on every public policy issue, regardless of whether or not it endeared him to Catholic voters. He properly rejected the concept that there was a Catholic position on every issue. His views on Red China, the Spanish Civil War, McCarthyism, peaceful coexistence with Soviet Russia, aid to Yugoslavia and Poland, a U.S. Ambassador to the Vatican, and aid to education were at odds with the majority sentiments within U.S. Catholicism. In November 1959 he said it would be wrong to refuse foreign aid to a country that used the funds for birth control programs.

During the campaign Kennedy kept his distance from clerical figures. He was privately disheartened that the Catholic hierarchy in Puerto Rico had ordered the faithful to oust Governor Munoz-Marin because of his liberal stand on birth control and divorce. Kennedy phoned Cardinal Cushing to see if he could intervene, but it was too late. Kennedy allegedly remarked, "Now I know why Henry VIII set up his own church."[29] More soberly, he worried: "If enough voters realize that Puerto Rico is a part of the United States, this could cost us the election."[30]

Even his relations with the Vatican were proper and detached. Kennedy was scheduled to visit the beloved Pope John during his European trip in June 1963, but the aged pontiff took ill and died. Kennedy offered to cancel that part of his trip, but Italian and Vatican authorities insisted that he come and meet the newly elected Pope, Paul VI. The President remained at Lake Como for an additional day so that his visit would not upstage the papal coronation.

His visit to the Pope on Tuesday had the press corps in a tizzy. Would the United States President kneel and kiss the papal ring? Kennedy told aides Dave Powers and Kenny O'Donnell that "Norman Vincent Peale would love that. And it would get me a lot of votes in South Carolina." He had never considered such a gesture because he was visiting the Vatican as a head of state, not as a Catholic layman. He clasped the Pope's hand and discussed international questions for a few minutes in the library at Clementine Hall. It would have been out of character for JFK to have done anything explicitly obeisant. He represented the United States at papal audiences precisely as Wilson and Eisenhower had done on previous occasions.[31]

On one occasion JFK expressed some sharply critical views of the hierarchy. "Naturally most of the hierarchy are extreme conservatives. They are accustomed to everyone's bowing down to them, to associating with the wealthiest men in the community. They like things as they are—they aren't going to be reformers."[32] (What would he have thought of Helder Camara?)

JFK challenged some of the sterile orthodoxies of his time, especially in regard to the reality and nature of the Communist "enemy." He categorically rejected the idea that Western democracy's bout with Communism was a "religious" one, with overtones of a moral crusade. This would have made Pope Pius XII cringe since the pontiff's opposition to Communism assumed the aura of a Holy War. Pius committed the Church to a posture of militancy against the Communist world and most Catholic statesmen, e.g., Adenauer, DeGaulle, Salazar, Franco, meekly obeyed. But not JFK.

Religious Humor

Observers as diverse as Kierkegaard and Elton Trueblood have long recognized the important symbolic value of religious humor. The ability to laugh at the foibles that exist in one's own religious tradition indicates at least a recognition of the flawed but lovable and common humanity basic to all people. It is also, most psychologists would agree, a healthy and mature attitude toward religion.

JFK was a master of religious humor. A few examples will suffice. During the 1960 campaign he urged President Truman to resist the temptation to send all Republicans to hell, admonishing the former President "not to raise the religious issue." In a 1959 address he responded to the question, "Can a Protestant be elected in 1960?" with this comment: "If he pledges absolute fidelity to the principle of separation of church and state, I don't see why he should be discriminated against." When asked if he thought all Protestants were heretics, he replied, "No, and I hope you don't think all Catholics are either." Similar stories are legion.

Kennedy's gentle and self-deprecating wit suggests a broad and tolerant approach to religion that is internally consistent with the other elements of his faith.

Some Unanswered Questions

At least three major questions continue to gnaw at many long-time Kennedy observers. One, how could JFK extricate himself from the devout Catholicism of his family and adopt policies or attitudes thoroughly at variance with the dominant Catholic ethos of his time? And, to what extent did his free-wheeling sexual adventurism (if true) represent rejection of stern Irish Catholic morality? Finally, how was he able to break with the historic Catholic understanding of church-state relations? Let us examine these dilemmas.

Some have suggested that Kennedy's independence is proof positive of a skin-deep or nominal attachment to Catholicism. I

cannot accept that interpretation on face value. Kennedy's secular
education, his appreciation of history, and his disinterest in Catholic social teaching played far more significant roles in the development of his character than his residual Catholicism. But Kennedy
did not see a strong conflict between the two. By the parochial,
insular standards of the Catholicism of his formative years, he
would not be considered a very good Catholic, it is true. But, as we
have seen, Kennedy rejected the concept that the Church had any
infallible prescriptions for the political or social dilemmas of the
world. Kennedy looked on religion generally as a mechanism for
improving interpersonal relations rather than resolving questions
that could properly be mitigated only by government.

It is possible that Kennedy's frequent disagreement with official
Church policies revealed endemic disbelief or rejection of his
religion, but it more likely reveals an impatience with the sluggish-
ness and uncreativity of the Church leadership. Kennedy was anti-
clerical and simply did not accord any special political wisdom to
the clergy. In many respects he approached the independent
Catholic of the post-Vatican II era, the "communal Catholic" of
which Andrew Greeley has written.

Greeley defines the communal Catholic as one who accepts his
religious heritage and refuses to jettison it for any other, simply
because there is no other religion that offers any more meaning.
But he resolutely refuses to believe that the Church leadership has
anything to say to him about political, social, economic, or even
sexual matters. To twist a metaphor a bit, the Catholic remains in
the Church but not of it. If JFK were alive today, he would be a
leading exponent of the communal Catholic principle. In that sense
Kennedy was something of a Catholic prophet. He accepted the
Church and some of its principles and values but he rejected its
claims to omnicompetence. If he was suspect during his lifetime, he
would be in the mainstream today.

We must also remember that Catholicism, despite its claims of
internal consistency and logical, continuous dogma, is susceptible
to many political interpretations. Despite the papal encyclicals of
Leo XIII and Pius XI and their attempt to develop a coherent
Catholic social philosophy for the twentieth century, Catholics

often harkened to the tune of a different drummer. (Ireland's great Catholic patriot Daniel O'Connell often stated that "we take our religion from Rome but our politics from home.")

Many European Catholics embraced socialism and supported social democratic and labor movements. (Today, there is a growing entente with Marxism in Latin America and Southern Europe.) An even greater number endorsed fascism and rightist nationalist movements. A Catholic propensity toward fascism was notable in Austria, Bavaria, Italy, Spain, Portugal, France, Croatia, Hungary, Poland, Slovakia, and elsewhere between the two World Wars. The idea that all Catholics should think alike politically, or that all should support the papacy or the local hierarchy on political matters was always held by more Protestant critics than individual Catholics. In the United States as well, a tremendous political diversity was always characteristic of Catholicism. Dorothy Day moved in one direction; Father Coughlin in another.

JFK's independence of spirit and willingness to dissent were not all that unusual, though it undoubtedly amazed most Protestants, who knew little or nothing about Catholics, and the loyalist minority of traditional or conservative Catholics.

In some respects JFK made dissent more respectable among Catholics in public life, though I think that the long-established American view that religion should not overtly influence politics has affected both Catholic and non-Catholic views—and still does to a great extent. Catholic members of Congress have consistently refused, by modest margins, to endorse adoption of a constitutional amendment banning abortion—though the hierarchy has demanded the change. Similarly, the nation's only Greek Orthodox governor, Michael Dukakis of Massachusetts, has vetoed anti-abortion legislation time and time again. He supports public funding of elective abortions for poor women, a widely unpopular position with the American public according to Gallup, Harris, and Yankelovich. His own Orthodox clergy are livid, having described abortion as a "heinous and unspeakable crime."

Protestants in politics pay little attention to church pronouncements. Although Baptists pay lip service to separation of church and state, Baptist officials blithely support compulsory prayer and

Bible reading in public schools in many communities and support anti-gambling and anti-drinking legislation wherever they have sufficient political power. In 1971, Baptist churchmen generally denounced the "prayer amendment" sponsored by Rep. Chalmers Wylie of Ohio. But 72 percent of Baptist Congressmen voted for the measure to overrule the Supreme Court's ban on compulsory prayer in public schools. Methodist and Presbyterian members of Congress ignored their church leaders' pleas and voted for the amendment by hefty margins.

The respected religious journalist Louis Cassels was a bit bemused by this effrontery. He wrote, "Passing resolutions, issuing pronouncements and adopting position statements on public issues is a major preoccupation of America's religious bodies. Actually, their impact on public policy, as a rule, ranges from the very slight to the indiscernible" (UPI, Jan. 17, 1972). Americans have always regarded clerical involvement in politics warily and have generally ignored preachers' political prescriptions. This is one of the prominent differentiating characteristics of the secular state.

Even President Jimmy Carter, who alone of recent Presidents seems to be allowing his personal religious sentiments to shape some public policies, has shown a willingness to break with Baptist tradition. In July 1977 he selected a Miami international lawyer, David Walters, as his personal envoy to the Vatican. This infuriated Southern Baptists, whose spokesmen and state newspapers denounced the action vigorously. Although most Americans (including Catholics) care little or nothing about this issue, Baptist papers made it front page news. Some, like the *Maryland Baptist*, indulged in nasty anti-Catholicism and called Carter a traitor. Jimmy Allen, a San Antonio preacher and President of the Southern Baptist Convention, denounced Carter, whom he had supported openly in 1976, and linked the Vatican envoy question to the Vatican school declaration, which implied that the world's governments should help finance parochial schools. Allen attacked the interference of "an Italian bishop" in American political affairs in language reminiscent of nineteenth century nativism. Yet, Mr. Carter felt that the value of an American voice at the politically sensitive and information-conscious Vatican outweighed the rancor

of his co-religionists. Carter critics should commend him for this move, even if they oppose the Vatican envoy, because it shows him unwilling to submit to clerical blackmail.

The second question I posed is a more difficult one to answer. If one accepts at face value the image of JFK as a lusty womanizer, whose leisure activities centered around the bedroom, the implications of rejection of Catholic morality are obvious. The problem is intensified by the necessity to evaluate the available evidence. So much of Kennedy's alleged promiscuity is based on hearsay, gossip, speculation, and the lurid revelations of call girls who want to make a quick buck that the serious biographer-historian is at a loss to know for sure. Kennedy-haters, of course, seize upon the scanty evidence with relish and glee. Victor Lasky's recent excursion into vile Kennedy-phobia devotes pages and pages to a retelling of the delicious details. I, for one, am not totally convinced about the veracity of these stories. I remain skeptical, as Adlai Stevenson did. But what if they are true? What kind of Catholic was he then?

Catholicism has always emphasized personal sexual purity and marital fidelity. It is a standard to which the faithful are expected to adhere. Human nature being what it is, the ideal is probably more honored in the breach than in the observance. Many may smirk about Kennedy and many pious, observant Catholics may be embarrassed, but his behavior, if true, does not exclude him from the Catholic fold. Prominent Catholics in public life have not always abided by the officially prescribed moral standards. Neither have Catholics of lesser prominence. Neither have Protestants, Orthodox, or other Christians been spotless. So to say that Kennedy's philandering automatically proves him to be a poor Catholic doesn't wash. It may prove that he was merely human.

When I mentioned this distasteful topic to a noted religious journalist and colleague of evangelical Protestant persuasion, I expected a leer and a prompt condemnation. I was surprised. He replied that we all have weaknesses and that we should not judge others harshly unless we know all the facts and circumstances surrounding JFK's relationship with his wife, the unusual circumstances of his career, and the psychological makeup which may have impelled him toward "illicit" sexual liaisons. I suspect that most Americans would prefer to leave Kennedy's love life to the

realm of speculation and concentrate on the truly significant and meaningful aspects of his character and career.

By the puritanical and moralistic standards of Irish-American Catholicism circa 1930, JFK was a pretty poor Catholic, an embarrassment, a "scandal" to the faithful. But by the pluralistic, conscience-oriented Catholicism of 1978, who is to say?

How did Kennedy arrive at the conclusion that church-state separation was an extraordinarily important concept? What intellectual processes led to the formation of his advocacy of a position known to be somewhat suspect by the Vatican and most U.S. bishops? Was he sincere, or was it political expediency that convinced him to adopt a separationist posture? Did his knowledge of history convince him of the reasonableness of the separationist approach?

Paul Blanshard, longtime foe of Catholic institutional interests, believes that Kennedy was sincerely committed to the principle without mental reservation. He (JFK) recognized in church-state separation a valuable insight of the American experience and a mechanism for the preservation of religious peace.[33]

John Cogley, prestigious Catholic journalist and advisor to Kennedy on church-state questions, concurs. "I think his answers were honest and forthright."[34]

Theodore Sorensen agreed. "He showed no awe of the Catholic hierarchy and no reservations about the widson of separating church and state."[35]

I am inclined to believe that JFK's commitment to separation was genuine and occurred early in his life. In 1937 young JFK, a student at Harvard, visited wartorn Spain and sent a communication to his father that is exceptionally revealing: "Their (the Republican government's) attitude toward the church was just a reaction to the strength of the Jesuits who had become much too powerful—the affiliation between church and state being much too close."[36]

Kennedy's perceptive view would have been denounced by Church officials and the diocesan press, which had been carrying on a verbal crusade for Franco since the Spanish Civil War began in 1936. Kennedy chose to evaluate historical events independently and did not accept an official Church line.

In February 1959 Senator Kennedy wrote in a letter to Glenn L.

Archer of Americans United: "It is my firm belief that there should be separation of church and state as we understand it in the United States—that is, that both church and state should be free to operate, without interference from each other in their respective areas of jurisdiction. We live in a liberal, democratic society which embraces wide varieties of belief and disbelief. There is no doubt in my mind that the pluralism which has developed under our Constitution, providing as it does a framework within which diverse opinions can exist side by side and by their interaction enrich the whole, is the most ideal system yet devised by man. I cannot conceive of a set of circumstances which would lead me to a different conclusion."[37]

Kennedy had by this time decided to seek the Presidency, so cynics might claim that the letter merely told Mr. Archer what Kennedy thought Archer wanted to hear. Kennedy's presidential record, though, confirms the views expressed in the letter.

Kennedy was not only sincere, in my judgment, but he rejected the belief that American Catholics could not in good conscience affirm complete acceptance of the church-state separation principle. (A view held by Paul Blanshard and the Vatican!) He wrote in 1959, "There is nothing inconsistent about believing in the separation of church and state and being a good Catholic."[38]

During the press conference following his September 12, 1960 address in Houston, Texas, Kennedy told a preacher who had suggested that the Vatican disapproved of his views that "I believe that I am stating the viewpoint that Catholics in this country hold toward that happy relationship which exists between church and state." When asked if he needed the approval of the Vatican, Kennedy replied, "I don't have to have approval."[39]

It is likely that JFK's knowledge of history, his secular education, and his contacts with thoughtful people of many faiths contributed to his acceptance of the separationist principle. One intellectual influence may have been John Courtney Murray, the American theologian whose advanced views on church-state relations were widely heralded as symptomatic of a new spirit in Catholicism. Murray challenged the traditional Catholic emphasis on full liberty only for "truth" and limited opportunity for "error." He also denied that a single Catholic philosophy of

church-state relations was valid for all societies, and urged that Catholics accept equality (not preferential treatment) in pluralistic cultures and grant equality to dissenters even in "Catholic states." His views were enunciated in the provocative *We Hold These Truths: Catholic Reflections on the American Proposition*, which appeared a few months before the 1960 election. Arthur Schlesinger, Jr. maintains that Kennedy's "basic attitude was wholly compatible with the sophisticated theology of Jesuits like Father John Courtney Murray, whom he greatly admired."[40]

Shortly before the dramatic Houston address, Theodore Sorensen read JFK's speech over the telephone to Father Murray, who approved. Some might question whether this was proper, but, as John Cogley remembers, Kennedy spoke to both Protestants and Catholics that night in Houston. He had to convince Protestants of his sincerity on church-state matters, but he could not disparage or distort the Catholic tradition for Catholic listeners.

It is significant that Father Murray considered Kennedy to be "far more of a separationist than I am."[41]

Kennedy and Murray were appropriate contemporaries. As *Newsweek*'s obituary on the death of Murray put it, "Murray demonstrated in theory what JFK demonstrated in practice: that Americanism and Roman Catholicism need no longer fear each other."[42]

James MacGregor Burns believed that Kennedy's "views on church and state stem from his belief in diversity, in heterogeneity, in pluralism."[43]

JFK, on one occasion, approached the different functions of church and state in a way which suggested that he understood the value of separation for genuine religious experience. In a January 29, 1950 address to the faculty and students at Notre Dame University (which had just bestowed an honorary degree on him), he said:

You have been taught that each individual has an immortal soul, composed of an intellect which can know truth and a will which is free. Because of this every Catholic must believe in the essential dignity of the human personality on which any democracy must rest. Believing this, Catholics can never adhere to any political theory which holds that the state is a separate, distinct organization to which allegiance must be paid rather than

a representative institution which derives its powers from the consent of the governed.

In addition, a Catholic's dual allegiance to the Kingdom of God on the one hand prohibits unquestioning obedience on the other to the state as an organic unit.[44]

JFK's view of the correct relationship between church and state is again exemplified by his position on an issue that emerged in the spring of 1960. The press had revealed that the U.S. Air Force was using a manual claiming that communism had infiltrated the country's Protestant churches and that seven thousand Protestant clergy were Communists. This charge was originally made by J. B. Mathews, a Methodist supporter of the late Senator Joseph McCarthy. Kennedy saw the charges as absurd and divisive. He said publicly that no church should try to dictate to the government and that the government should neither favor nor oppose any church.

Kennedy decried the Air Force manual and called for its removal in these words:

No church should undertake to impose its views on public agencies, and no public agency should single out for attack any church or organization.

Under the First Amendment our Government cannot—directly or indirectly, carelessly or intentionally—select any religious body for either favorable or unfavorable treatment.

Thanks to the protest of Kennedy and others, the discredited manual was discontinued.[45]

Kennedy's commitment to separation was genuine, a reflection of his secular education, his sense of history, and his rejection of religion's ability to communicate any unique political, economic, or social insights. To him religion belonged in the sanctuary, not the legislative halls.

Cardinal Cushing, when asked if he considered Kennedy a practicing Catholic, responded, "He was just as good a Catholic as I am, and he had ideas similar to mine. I don't like to parade my religion. I try to live as I'm supposed to live. He was the same."[46] Cushing's personal friendship for Kennedy may have colored his interpretation and made it too irenic. But I wonder if the crusty, humane, and sagacious old Cardinal didn't have a point.

Too much is made of pious proclamations and too little of genuine ethical behavior. Kennedy considered himself a Catholic with a conscience, an autonomous, intelligent human being who made decisions in accordance with that conscience. He remained a part of his religious heritage and operated within its parameters. He chose not to reject it as Eugene O'Neill and F. Scott Fitzgerald had done. (Perhaps it is easier for novelists than for politicians to lose one's faith in public.)

To answer the question I posed in the introduction: Neither Rose Kennedy nor James Reston is completely right.

Kennedy was not a fully observant, old-school Catholic. But neither did he "disbelieve" in the tenets of his faith nor did he ignore them. He was a man for many, if not all, seasons. He was, and should be remembered as, a Catholic statesman and a democratic humanist, a man who exemplified the best in the Catholic and American traditions.

Notes

1. *Time*, 27 April 1959.
2. Clay Blair, Jr. and Joan Blair, *The Search for JFK* (New York: Berkley Publishing Corp., 1976), pp. 11, 184.
3. Evelyn Lincoln's files, Kennedy Library.
4. Theodore Sorensen, *Kennedy* (New York: Harper & Row, 1965), p. 19.
5. Ibid.
6. Oral interview with Dean Francis Sayre, Kennedy Library.
7. Lawrence B. Fuchs, *John F. Kennedy and American Catholicism* (Meredith Press, 1967), p. 249.
8. Ibid., p. 229.
9. Ibid., p. 168.
10. Kenneth O'Donnell and David F. Powers, *Johnny, We Hardly Knew Ye* (New York: Pocket Books, 1976), p. 478.
11. See *Christian Herald*, December 1959, February 1960, April 1960.
12. Oral interview with Dean Francis Sayre, Kennedy Library.
13. Oral interview with Dean Francis Sayre, Kennedy Library.
14. Oral interview with Dean Francis Sayre, Kennedy Library.
15. James MacGregor Burns, *John Kennedy: A Political Profile* (New York: Harcourt Brace Jovanovich, Inc., 1960), p. 249.

16. Kathleen Rowland, "Mr. Kennedy Didn't Want Any Fuss," in *The Universe Book, 1965*, ed. Piers Compton (London: Robert Hale, 1964), pp. 170-172.

17. Fuchs, *Kennedy and American Catholicism*, p. 207.

18. Sorensen, *Kennedy*, p. 126.

19. Ibid.

20. Oral interview with Brooks Hays, Kennedy Library.

21. Oral interview with Brooks Hays, Kennedy Library.

22. White House Central Files, Kennedy Library.

23. Burns, *John Kennedy*, p. 249.

24. Oral interview with Brooks Hays, Kennedy Library.

25. Oral interview with Cardinal Cushing, Kennedy Library.

26. Fuchs, *Kennedy and American Catholicism*, p. 164.

27. Ibid., p. 206.

28. Ibid., p. 207.

29. Sorensen, *Kennedy*, p. 148.

30. O'Donnell and Powers, *Johnny, We Hardly Knew Ye*, pp. 249-250.

31. Ibid., p. 432.

32. Sorensen, *Kennedy*, p. 112.

33. Personal interview with Mr. Blanshard, 16 January 1977.

34. John Cogley, *A Canterbury Tale: Experiences & Reflections: 1916-1976* (New York: Seabury Press, 1976), p. 85.

35. Sorensen, *Kennedy*, p. 19.

36. Quoted in Herbert L. Matthews, *Half of Spain Died* (New York: Charles Scribner's Sons, 1973), p. 119.

37. Americans United archives, Silver Spring, Maryland.

38. Sorensen, *Kennedy*, p. 19.

39. Fuchs, *Kennedy and American Catholicism*, p. 181.

40. Arthur M. Schlesinger, Jr., *A Thousand Days: John F. Kennedy in the White House* (Boston: Houghton Mifflin Co., 1965), p. 108.

41. Father John Courtney Murray to Mrs. J. M. Dewine, 19 May 1967, in Murray papers at Woodstock College.

42. John Courtney Murray, "The Voice of Reason," *Newsweek*, 28 August 1967.

43. Burns, *John Kennedy*, p. 250.

44. Ibid., p. 242.

45. *New York Times*, 18 April 1960.

46. Oral interview with Cardinal Cushing, Kennedy Library.

Chapter 5
PRESIDENTIAL RELIGION

How religious do Americans want their presidents to be and how religious have they, in fact, been? These are some questions that we need to answer before placing John F. Kennedy in the religious spectrum of presidential religion.

There seems to be a consensus that most Americans, even religiously indifferent ones, want their Presidents to have at least a veneer of religion, however insincere that religion may be to the President himself. When I asked election specialist Richard Scammon this question, he replied: "It is safer for candidates to have at least some religious commitment."[1]

William Burlie Brown, in his uniquely fascinating and valuable study of the campaign biography as a literary form, concludes that there is a distinct pattern to the religion espoused by presidential candidates. "From 1824 to 1960 there is a remarkable consistency on the subject of the candidate's religion. He is deeply reverent but never sanctimonious. Although he is an 'orthodox Christian,' he is not narrowly sectarian. Above all he is tolerant—a firm believer in religious freedom." He cautions: "There is a vagueness about the handling of the candidates' religious faith...but this vagueness does not emanate from any design to deceive. It is, rather, that sincere vagueness that appears to be endemic to religion in America—a nation that has spawned the most sects and the fewest theologians."[2]

Brown suggests that all the presidents have expressed some belief in God, a view echoed by Richard Scammon and others who feel that an aggressive nonbeliever would have a difficult time being elected in the United States. Brown also believes that presidential religion has been essentially nonsectarian, though vaguely Protestant. He says: "In essence the principle that can be extracted from countless expressions on the subject in the campaign biographies boils down to this: religion is only a personal matter between each man and God in so far as it involves a choice of a Christian sect; but while it is important that such a choice be made, it does not matter which sect is chosen."³ Finally, Brown suggests that religious tolerance is essential to a presidential candidate.

Several candidates spoke out against religious bigotry and intolerance, primarily relating to Roman Catholics. Theodore Roosevelt, on one occasion, specifically mentioned his admiration for Jews. Religious tolerance, then, along with honesty, generosity, and integrity are seen to be important values to prospective American presidents.

Another point that can be made is that the public man in America has generally been uninterested in religion and theologically uninformed. With the exception of Jefferson, the Adamses, Wilson, and Lincoln, America's presidents have been remarkably uninterested in religion. A certain reticence about religious discussion can also be seen in presidential autobiographies.

Historian Robert S. Alley has categorized our presidents into three distinct religious traditions:

Type A includes those in the Congregational-Unitarian tradition, with its emphasis on enlightened humanism; they were "goal-oriented" in approach, "vigorously repudiating the restrictive proclivities" of institutional religion. These are the church-state separationists who gave us the First Amendment, men such as John Adams, Jefferson, Madison, John Quincy Adams, and Lincoln.

Type B are the legalistic Calvinists, who propounded and implemented the messianic concept of government. Those in this tradition felt that "national success was dependent upon a national righteousness." Alley says that this "Calvinism sought to implement a king's chapel in a king's court without the religious establishment." Presidents of this type include Jackson, Grant,

Cleveland, McKinley, Theodore Roosevelt, Wilson, Harding, Coolidge, Hoover, Truman, Eisenhower, Johnson, and Nixon.

Type C are the Anglican-Catholic pragmatic idealists, who emphasized realism and situation ethics. These presidents, such as Washington, Pierce, Arthur, Franklin Roosevelt, and Kennedy, "viewed politics and religion in perfect harmony, each within its own sphere." This approach "takes the institutions of religion seriously, positively." Freed of narrow orthodoxy or utopian ideologizing, "the third way is one that allows for freedom in movement from church to state and back again."[4]

As one reads the literature of presidential religion carefully, one encounters a very basic flaw, one which adds to the difficulty of discovering reliable, credible material. Most of the writings on presidential religion have sought to conform the president to the image that the author held. A number of studies attempted to show that all of America's Presidents were God-fearing, pious, deeply religious men. Examples of this mold include Louis A. Banks's 1902 book, *The Religious Life of Famous Americans*; *The Religious Faith of Great Men* by Archer Wallace (1935); and *The Presidents: Men of Faith* by Bliss Isely, published in 1953. In his preface, Isely stated: "In comparison with other nations, the United States has been fortunate in its chief executives. The mother of one President was a minister. The fathers of three others were clergymen. Five married parsonage-born women. One president was a clergyman and filled a regular charge. Another often filled a pulpit. Two, while colonels in the army, doubled as chaplains. Two others studied for the ministry. A large percentage served as church officers or church school leaders."[5]

Presbyterian pastor John Sutherland Bonnell, for many years pastor of the prestigious Fifth Avenue Presbyterian Church in New York, made similar claims in his 1971 book, *Presidential Profiles: Religion in the Life of American Presidents*. In it he claimed, "Americans are basically a religious people. They also expect their Presidents to manifest a religious faith. ...the thirty-six men who have served this nation as President have indeed been men of faith. Without a single exception, at one time or another, they have all publicly avowed their trust in God."[6] Bonnell was impressed by the fact that many of the presidents enjoyed reading the Bible. He said:

"One had read it at least once from cover to cover, and one resolved to do this annually. One compiled a scholarly selection of the moral teaching of Jesus. ... As one studies the lives of the Presidents, it would seem as though Providence had conspired to give them religious associations."[7]

Another example of this type of eisegesis is *The Presidents and the Bible* by J. W. Storer. Originally published by Broadman Press in 1952, a new edition was brought out in 1976. In this study Storer, a Baptist minister, selected the scripture passages used at the inaugurations of Presidents Lincoln through Ford and attempted to prove that selection of a particular Biblical verse showed that all of our presidents were devoutly religious. Storer said that he had "no doubt that each of our Presidents selected a scripture passage with real feeling and that it was with deep humility that he bowed his head and pressed to his lips the Word of God."[8]

Other examples of this genre include Christian F. Reisner's *Roosevelt's Religion* (Abingdon Press, 1924), a study of Theodore Roosevelt, William Judson Hampton's *The Religion of the Presidents,* and Vernon B. Hampton's *The Religious Background of the White House.* The common theme of these books was that all the American Presidents fit a preconceived mold of political religiosity.

Skeptics and freethinkers have not been without their flaws, however. Franklin B. Steiner's *Religious Beliefs of Our Presidents* attempted to show that most of our presidents were actually skeptical men who rejected the basic moral and ethical foundations and supernatural elements of Christianity. Likewise, Steiner and Joseph McCabe in *Seven Infidel Presidents* tended to select evidence that was sketchy and to ignore evidence that would refute their thesis. They, too, tended to use omission of presidential religiousness as prima facie evidence of irreligion. They were guilty of a desire to see the presidents as images of their own orientation.

Fortunately, there have been a few studies that ignored prefabricated opinions and sought to discern the truth about the religious opinions of the individual occupants of the White House. Some of these works add significantly to our knowledge.

Instead of attempting to prove that a president was either very religious or not at all religious, they investigated the President's religious life and let the chips fall where they may. Edmund Fuller

and David Green's *God in the White House* is a good example of this approach. They stress the irony of the intense American interest in the religion of the chief executive, while the Constitution legally forbids religious tests for public office and separates the institutions of church and state. "With characteristic human illogic, the American people always have been interested in the religious beliefs of their Presidents—some of them passionately so. Pulpit, platform, press, books and conversation have been absorbed with the subject from time to time."[9] The contrast with England is instructive. That nation has an established church, but its citizens would be hard put to even identify the religious affiliation or belief of recent Prime Ministers. Religious affiliation apparently holds no interest for the British public or press.

Some of the more prominent studies which objectively evaluate presidential religion include Paul F. Boller's *George Washington and Religion,* Charles P. Henderson's *The Nixon Theology,* William Lee Miller's *Piety Along the Potomac,* and Norman Cousin's splendid *In God We Trust: The Religious Beliefs and Ideas of the American Founding Fathers.*

More has been written about Abraham Lincoln's religion than about any other president. The Library of Congress lists over fifty titles, and one new one, G. Frederick Owen's *A Heart That Yearned For God,* was issued by Third Century Publishers in late 1976. Once again the dichotomy appears. Attempts have been made to "prove" that Lincoln fit into a certain theological mold. The ambiguity, complexity, and depth of Lincoln's religion are factors helping to sustain the widespread interest in it. Among the more objective and intellectually reputable studies are Elton Trueblood's *Abraham Lincoln: Theologian of American Anguish,* William J. Wolf's *The Almost Chosen People,* and William E. Barton's *The Soul of Abraham Lincoln.* Barton's is still considered, after fifty-seven years, the preeminent classic in the field. *Lincoln's Religion,* a collection of sources edited by Douglas C. McMurtrie in 1936, is also valuable.

Attempts to show that Lincoln was thoroughly secular and anti-religious include his early law partner William Herndon's *Life of Lincoln* and John E. Remsburg's *Six Historic Americans,* which devotes over three hundred pages to Lincoln.

Pietistic, hagiographic studies of Lincoln are legion and include William J. Johnstone's *Abraham Lincoln: The Christian,* John Wesley Hill's *Abraham Lincoln, Man of God,* Ervin Chapman's *Latest Light of Lincoln,* Willard L. Sperry's *The Meaning of God in the Life of Lincoln,* H. H. Horner's *The Growth of Lincoln's Faith,* and Ralph Lindstrom's *Lincoln Finds God.*

Two specialized treatments worth consulting are Edgar DeWitt Jones's *Lincoln and the Preachers,* and Clarence McCartney's *Lincoln and the Bible.* About all one can conclude is that Lincoln knew the Bible better than any other president and was interested in the moral and ethical aspects of Christianity and very uninterested in its dogmatic and ecclesiastical aspects.

Is it at all possible to make any credible generalizations about presidential religion? It would seem that a few defensible statements could be made. (1) Though a majority of our presidents (twenty-one out of thirty-nine) have been Episcopalians, Presbyterians, or Methodists, there is little denominational attachment. There is a rather nominal identification. (2) Church attendance has been moderate, though modern presidents have been careful to be photographed attending various churches (especially near election time). The earlier presidents tended to downplay public religiosity, and Presidents Jackson, Pierce, and Polk refused to join any churches during their Presidency in order to avoid charges that they were using religion for political gain. (3) Almost all have been rather tolerant men and openly urged respect for different religious tradition. Some anti-Catholic prejudice has been attributed to John Adams, Fillmore, Grant, Garfield, and Hayes, and anti-Semitism to Grant, but they were relatively minor facets of their public careers. (Jefferson was quite critical of all churches, and especially of the clergy.) No president has ever sought to legally repress any religious group. (4) Very few of them gave evidence of any strong intellectual interests in religion, which is not at all unusual. As Fuller and Green noted: "Though some of our Presidents unquestionably have been men of deeply religious nature and commitment, in their own terms, others have been indifferent to the subject. This is not surprising. In general the temperament, career patterns, and attributes of mind likely to lead a man to the Presidency are not those of a man inclined to dwell much on religion. It

is more surprising that some of our Presidents have actively interested themselves in religion than that a few others have not."[10] Finally, all of our presidents have accepted the principles of religious liberty and separation of church and state. This is hardly surprising, as this concept is so ingrained in the American experience as to constitute the most genuine and creative contribution of the U.S.A. to political theory and jurisprudence.

How does JFK compare with recent presidents? With Nixon and Carter, for example?

The religious contrast between Kennedy and Nixon is quite revealing. Whereas Kennedy was open and generous, Nixon was secretive and niggardly. Let me explain. During his presidency Richard M. Nixon held a well-publicized series of White House religious services, all calculated to trumpet the moral tone of his White House. Carefully selected preachers came to deliver the message. A study of *White House Sermons* (Harper & Row, 1972) shows a preponderance of escapist, vapid, and obtuse moralizing and simplistic theology. Nixon favorites Norman Vincent Peale, Billy Graham, and Cardinal John Krol gave repeat performances. There were no Episcopalians, United Church of Christ, or Unitarian participants, and there was not a hint of prophetic preaching in the sermons delivered during the first term. John F. Kennedy would never have dared such effrontery. He worshipped quietly, mostly at nearby St. Stephen Martyr Church or at the local parishes in Hyannisport or Palm Beach.

Secondly, Richard M. Nixon was smugly horrified at the suggestion of presidential profanity. In one of the Kennedy-Nixon debates, Nixon made sophisticated and knowledgeable people retch when he denounced former President Truman's occasional public "damn" and "hell" and told television viewers that he was proud of President Eisenhower's virginal tongue. Insiders must have had a hearty laugh, since old soldier Ike was known for hard swearing. What really galls, though, is Nixon's hypocrisy. The Watergate tapes revealed an almost unending stream of profanity and invective, engaged in by President Nixon. Evangelicals, especially, hit the ceiling when the contents of those sordid conversations were revealed. Reverend Pat Robertson of the Christian Broadcasting Network called on Nixon to apologize to the Christians of America.

Kennedy, of course, swore heartily but he made no bones about it. To him it was a natural but not necessarily enviable habit acquired by men in public life. He even joked about it during the Al Smith dinner in 1960, telling the audience an anecdote about a Nixon address the day before. In this tale Nixon swears like a sailor in order to elicit a juicy campaign contribution.

Nixon's attempt to cheat on his income taxes in the late 1960s and early 1970s reveals another contrast with Kennedy. Nixon claimed to be an evangelical who was "saved" at a tent rally during his youth. (See his article in *Decision*, the Billy Graham Evangelistic Association monthly, November, 1962.) As an evangelical he was supposed to be generous in his stewardship of financial resources. His tax record showed that less than one half of one percent of his income was donated to any charity, religious or otherwise. This would have been unthinkable to most evangelicals. JFK gave his entire salary to a wide variety of charities, but did so in a spirit of anonymity. JFK also gave the royalties of his best-selling *Profiles in Courage* to a religious charity.

What about John F. Kennedy and Jimmy Carter? There are a number of similarities between President Carter and President Kennedy. Among them: (1) Both were young, dynamic challengers seeking to oust rather stodgy, unimaginative incumbents (or quasi-incumbents). (2) Both had a major handicap: Kennedy's Catholicism and Carter's Southern origin. Their elections broke long-standing taboos that had tarnished American democracy. (3) The religious issue was raised against both in a virulent way—though it was much more severe in Kennedy's case, where Article VI was in real danger of violation. In Carter's campaign, however, the Republican Party was directly involved in religious slander. Some of the same notorious bigots opposed both candidates. (4) Millions of votes shifted from normal party allegiances because of religion. On balance, Kennedy lost more and Carter gained slightly because of it. (5) The coalitions of both were roughly similar: Catholics, Jews, blacks, labor, and the South. A majority of Kennedy states went for Carter and vice versa. (Of course, both were Democrats.) (6) Both offered hope of genuine change, vigor, excitement, and a recovery of lost faith in our national institutions.

But there are some differences, too. (1) Kennedy was an insider, having served in Congress for fourteen years. Carter is the archetypical outsider, who surfaced on the national political scene with unwonted suddenness and captivated the electorate (at least 51 percent of it). (2) Kennedy was an authentic spellbinder, an eloquent orator. Carter is not. (3) JFK frequently quoted the Bible in public addresses, but Carter rarely does so. JFK's use of the Bible was literary and hortatorical, while Carter seems to approach it devotionally and meditatively. (4) The most obvious difference was Kennedy's refusal to discuss his personal religious faith. Carter, in contrast, seems to relish the opportunity to "witness" for his faith and has left himself open to charges of religious exhibitionism and using religion for political gain.

JFK would have been wryly amused and somewhat incredulous at Carter's willingness to reveal his innermost religious thoughts and convictions, but he would probably have defended Carter's right to do so. Kennedy would caution Carter about the political consequences of overt religious identification. Ironically, Catholic Kennedy and Baptist Truman were much closer in their views about mixing politics and religion than either is to Carter. One can scarcely conceive of Harry Truman's telling a political audience that he is a born-again Christian who prays frequently and reads the Bible in Spanish. Truman told the public, "I am a Baptist. Period." His religious views were a private matter and he preferred to keep it that way.

How has the influence of religion on politics changed since the Kennedy Presidency? And how has Jimmy Carter's handling of religion-as-a-political-issue affected the shape of the church-state debate?

For one thing, vehement anti-Catholicism has declined considerably. No serious religious objections were raised against Eugene McCarthy or Robert Kennedy in the 1968 Democratic nomination battle. The nomination of a Catholic for vice president was almost institutionalized with Republican William Miller in 1964, and Democrats Edmund Muskie in 1968 and Sargent Shriver in 1972. Some prejudice still exists, especially among Southern Protestants. A 1969 Gallup Poll found that 8 percent of the electorate would

still refuse to vote for a well-qualified Catholic or Jewish Presidential candidate. A 1976 Lou Harris survey revealed that 20 percent of Americans opposed a Jewish vice president and 12 percent were against a Catholic's holding that office. Bigotry dies hard in America.

In general, though, religious influences on politics have become more sophisticated and issue-oriented. Both major political parties have at times made explicit appeals to certain religious groups. In recent years, beginning with the 1964 Goldwater campaign, the Republican Party platforms have endorsed constitutional amendments to restore prayer and Bible reading to public schools and supported some type of aid to parochial and private school patrons. In 1976 the GOP adopted a rather strong anti-abortion plank in an attempt to garner so-called "right to life" votes. The GOP strategy was to win a higher percentage than normal of the pivotal Catholic vote (23 to 25 percent of the electorate) and to solidify the party's historic appeal to evangelical Protestants (20 percent of the electorate). The results of this strategy are mixed but generally unproductive and disappointing.

During the 1976 primaries "the religious issue" surfaced once again after Georgia's former Governor Jimmy Carter told audiences that he was a "born-again Christian" whose life had been transformed by a deep religious experience in 1966 or 1967. This electrified many evangelical and Protestant audiences, and Carter ran well in evangelical counties in Florida, North Carolina, Ohio, Pennsylvania, Michigan, Maryland, and elsewhere. His frequent discussion of his personal religious sentiment, however, began to frighten many Jews, Catholics, and nonreligious liberals.

Was he a dangerous religious fanatic? Would he discriminate in favor of fellow Baptists and evangelicals? Did his rural Southern upbringing predispose him against Northern urban Catholics and Jews? Were evangelicals using him as a way to regain their lost political power and would they repress and persecute Catholics, Jews, and liberals as they had done in some areas from 1850 to 1930? These fears intensified during the primaries. Carter ran poorly among Jews, who favored Jackson, Udall, or Brown. Catholic areas went for Brown or Udall generally. Carter ran poorly in states with few evangelical voters (New York, Massachu-

setts, Oregon, Rhode Island).

Carter, after his nomination, sought to counter the fears of nonevangelicals by assiduously courting Jewish and Catholic voters. Although adopting a rather equivocal stance on abortion, which hurt among some Catholics, Carter sought big city Catholic votes on traditional bread-and-butter and family issues. Much of the Catholic press was moderately hostile to Carter and embittered about the abortion plank in the party platform, which opposed an anti-abortion constitutional amendment. The Democrats also failed to support parochial school aid or prayer in the schools, issues that have appeal to a segment of the conservative electorate. (A significant percentage of the liberal and moderate Jewish and Protestant community vigorously opposes aid to church schools and compulsory religion in public schools.)

The underdog Republicans saw a grand opportunity to effect a realignment along these issues and courted the normally Democratic Catholic and Jewish constituencies as fervently, or more so, than Nixon had done in 1972. The Catholic bishops met with both candidates but expressed a strong preference for the Republican position on abortion, a move interpreted as pro-Ford. Anti-abortion activists plagued the Carter-Mondale campaign from the start. One Ford aide told *Newsweek* that the Republicans would even seek votes by appealing to the "cultural combativeness" between Baptists and Catholics in such states as Texas, Missouri, Louisiana, and Kentucky. (Presumably, this meant appealing to Catholics, not Baptists.)

The evangelicals and Baptists were a problem for the GOP because so many were switching to Carter. Evangelical publishers brought out *The Miracle of Jimmy Carter* and other adulatory volumes. Disillusionment over Nixon's hypocrisy (swearing, income tax cheating, lack of stewardship, toleration of corruption) threatened to produce a Democratic majority among evangelicals for the first time in history. (Neither FDR nor LBJ had won a majority.) Baptist state newspapers felt resentment at the attacks on Carter during the primaries and expressed much pride in his nomination, though remaining officially neutral. Then Carter gave them a jolt with the *Playboy* interview.

The mid-campaign bombshell hurt Carter among puritanical

evangelicals, many of whom expressed dismay and shock. His candid views on adultery and personal pride resulted in a spate of evangelical defections and open endorsements of the Ford-Dole team. Led by Baptist pastor W. A. Criswell of Dallas, Texas, who bitterly fought Kennedy in 1960, many notable evangelicals switched back to Ford, himself an evangelical conservative. Many of the same preachers who battled JFK now denounced Carter, leading many to wonder if their basic political conservatism was reasserting itself.

The President Ford Committee seized on this fumble and sent out three to four million pieces of campaign literature designed for rural evangelical voters. Called *Heartland*, this four-page newsletter called Carter a religious hypocrite and a fraud, while depicting Ford as a great man who relied on Holy Scripture. The evangelical drift back to Ford made this election a whole new ball game, though it must be noted that many religious leaders defended the content of Mr. Carter's *Playboy* interview, noting that it was theologically sound and compassionate. On balance, polls showed the interview to be hurting Carter, though among religiously nonaffiliated voters Carter was perceived more favorably.

In the campaign's closing days, Senator Robert Dole pounded these church-state religiocultural themes and added a curious new one: church tax exemptions. Dole claimed that Carter favored taxing church-owned commercial property and business enterprises, which, Dole said, would destroy religious freedom. Dole spent so much time in the Catholic strongholds of Southern Louisiana that some observers wondered what office he was seeking.

As the results poured in, it was clear that some religious realignment was occurring. Carter lost heavily Catholic Connecticut and New Jersey and was running below the Democratic norm in Rhode Island and Massachusetts. But he was sweeping the South and border states and nine of the ten most heavily Baptist states. He was also winning record votes in Lutheran areas of Minnesota and Wisconsin and doing well in other Catholic strongholds, including south Louisiana, northern New Mexico, south Texas and some of the German-American bailiwicks of the Midwest. A close examination of tightly contested Ohio, Pennsylvania, and Missouri indicated that Carter's gains in Protestant counties offset losses in

Catholic areas and enabled him to carry those states. A new coalition was being born.

Jimmy Carter's narrow victory over President Ford reveals some fascinating realignments. Put bluntly, both candidates were modestly successful in raiding the other's historic bases. Carter ran better among Protestants than is normal for Democrats, but less well among Catholics and Jews. CBS news and Gallup gave Carter 46 percent of the Protestant vote, a gain of 7 percent over the 1952-1972 average Democratic Presidential vote among Protestants. Among Catholics, Carter's 55 percent was 6 percent below par, while his 68 percent Jewish vote was 11 percent below the Democratic norm during the same period. Carter carried fifteen of the seventeen heaviest evangelical states, narrowly failing only in Oklahoma and Virginia. His extraordinary showing in southern Illinois, Indiana, and Ohio, and in central and southern Pennsylvania suggests that the Protestant vote was crucial to his election. Carter carried or almost carried several Ohio and Pennsylvania Protestant strongholds lost by Kennedy and Humphrey.

Did Carter's religion help or hurt on balance? In the absence of scientific motivational analysis, we cannot know for sure, but I am inclined to think it helped a little more than it hurt. A Gallup poll in October found, for example, that 20 percent of voters were favorably impressed (in a political sense) by Carter's religion, compared to 10 percent of voters who were unfavorably affected, and 70 percent claimed to ignore his religion's politcal salience. His Protestant gains outdistanced Catholic and Jewish losses, though the fluctuation and movement varied in each state.

Although Carter made strong promises that he would not allow his personal religion to influence his public policies, there have already been a few eyebrow-raising events.

At Carter's inaugural ceremony it was decided (by whom is still uncertain) that the clergy who offer prayers should be cut from four to two. Protestant and Catholic clergy have long been included. A rabbi has participated since the Roosevelt-Truman days, and a Greek Orthodox prelate has been present since Eisenhower's second inaugural. The Carter staff decided to drop the Jewish and Eastern Orthodox representatives, an action that resulted in criticism. Carter was accused of insensitivity toward two religious

minorities, whose members had worked hard to erase prejudice and misunderstanding and who interpreted the exclusion as a slight. At the least it was surely a political error. Defenders of Carter, including some separationists, supported the action as a laudable attempt to reduce some of the civil religion attendant upon the inaugural ceremonies. Unfortunately, once something is institutionalized, it is difficult to change without hurting feelings, and the Jews and Orthodox acutely felt their minority status once again.

In June 1977 President Carter invited a group of Baptist missionaries to the White House and encouraged them to expand their efforts "to reach the world for Christ." JFK would never have thought of inviting Catholic missionaries to the White House. He would have considered it inappropriate. It would have been unthinkable anyway, since the wrath of Baptists and other Protestants would have fallen on him. The fact that Carter can get away with it, without a murmur of dissent from normally hard-line separationists, suggests either (1) that the ecumenical movement has silenced most opposition to this type of mixing religion and politics, or (2) that evangelical Protestantism is indeed the American "established" religion.

Carter's teaching of Sunday School at Washington's First Baptist Church has not only increased class attendance but also sent normally pagan journalists there in search of wisdom and enlightenment. Some have questioned this behavior and suggested that Carter needs to be seen as President of all the people. Some church-state specialists vehemently disagree. Edd Doerr, editor of *Church & State*, says that the free exercise clause of the First Amendment protects a president's religious practice, however overt or visible it may be. "If the President can't practice his religion, who can?" he asks.

On two substantive, as opposed to symbolic, issues Mr. Carter has taken positions directly resulting from his religious understanding. Abortion is one. This contentious issue, more than any other one perhaps, seems most susceptible to religious interpretation since the origin, nature, and purpose of life are seen to be at stake. Carter, though recognizing that abortion is now a legally protected option, has vigorously opposed government funding of all but the most medically crucial procedures. This is, of course, the Supreme

Court's view and the dominant view in the nation. He has drawn attention to the moral and religious aspects, though, and has stated his opposition on the grounds that many people have strong moral objections to government encouragement of elective abortions resulting from capriciousness or promiscuity.

At a press conference in the summer of 1977 Carter made one of the most revealing statements of his career. When asked if it was fair that rich women could always obtain abortions but that poor women were dependent on Medicaid for the same procedure, Carter replied that there is much in life that is unfair. He told a questioner at his July 13 press conference, "There are many things in life that are not fair, that wealthy people can afford and poor people cannot. But I don't believe that the federal government should take action to try to make these opportunities exactly equal, particularly when there is a moral factor involved." He elaborated on this view and provoked much discussion during the following weeks. Some commended his realism, his recognition of the "tragic sense of life." Others, including many liberal Christians, wondered aloud if the function of government was not primarily designed to make life less unfair for the downtrodden and unprivileged sectors of society. After all, had not Mr. Carter frequently quoted Niebuhr on the necessity of trying to bring about justice in a sinful and unjust world? Whatever the final outcome of this donnybrook will be, the incident shows that Carter accepts the morose Southern Baptist worldview—one traditionally held by the déclassé and impoverished fundamentalists and by many fatalistic Roman Catholics in the Irish and Latin cultures.

Carter's "life is unfair" statement is similar to one attributed to JFK, but it is difficult to compare the context since Kennedy's views on abortion are unknown. I rather suspect, though, that Kennedy would have been very careful not to inject his personal religious sentiments into this issue but would have tried to approach it as a public policy question without reference to theology. But I am only speculating.

On the question of the survival of the state of Israel, Mr. Carter has evoked an apocalyptic-theological view that astounds many observers. During the campaign and in meeting with Jewish leaders since his election, Carter has said that he believes modern Israel to

be "the fulfillment of Biblical prophecy because God wants the Jewish people to have a place to live." Most Jews would probably prefer that a U.S. President's support for Israel be based on political rather than theological considerations. Carter's view, though, is representative of a segment of conservative Protestantism.

A number of prominent evangelicals took out a full page ad in the *Washington Post* on November 1, 1977. Boldly entitled "Evangelicals Concern for Israel," the ad stated, in part, "We affirm as Evangelicals our belief in the promise of the land to the Jewish people—a promise first made to Abraham and repeated throughout Scripture, a promise which has never been abrogated. We believe the rebirth of Israel as a nation and the return of her people to the land is clearly foretold in the Bible and this fulfillment in our time is one of the most momentous events in all human history." The statement concluded, "The time has come for Evangelical Christians to affirm their belief in biblical prophecy and Israel's Divine Right to the Land."

This invocation of theological presupposition to determine foreign policy is a clear departure from the norm. If Carter proceeds in this direction, it will have many ramifications for the future. To John Kennedy it would have been mystifying, if not unthinkable.

In no way do I criticize this increasing Christian concern for Israel. In many respects it is a welcome development, signaling the demise of anti-Semitism. It may represent an attempt to purge some of the guilt many Christians feel today for the relative inaction of their predecessors toward the suffering Jews during the Holocaust. But many sincere and thoughtful Americans question to what extent foreign policy should be based on theology.

In summary, then, it is ironic that Kennedy's quiet, reserved Catholicism was very much in the mainstream of what I have chosen to call "Presidential" religion. It was tolerant, pragmatic, flexible, vague, and—most important of all—tidily compartmentalized and rarely expressed in public. And this is the way most Americans seem to prefer it, Jimmy Carter notwithstanding.

Notes

1. Interview on "Religion and Politics in the 1970's," *Church & State,* May 1973.

2. William Burlie Brown, *The Peoples Choice* (Baton Rouge: Louisiana State University Press, 1960), pp. 130-131.

3. Ibid.

4. Robert S. Alley, *So Help Me God* (Atlanta: John Knox Press, 1972), pp. 24-27.

5. Bliss Iseley, *The Presidents: Men of Faith* (Boston: W. A. Wilde Company, 1953).

6. John Sutherland Bonnell, *Presidential Profiles: Religion in the Life of American Presidents* (Philadelphia: Westminster Press, 1971), p. 13.

7. Ibid., p. 14.

8. J. W. Storer, *The Presidents and the Bible* (Nashville: Broadman Press, 1952), p. v, vi.

9. Edmund Fuller and David Green, *God in the White House* (New York: Crown Publishers Inc., 1968), p. 2.

10. Fuller and Green, *God in the White House*, pp. 4-5; see also, Albert J. Menendez, *Religion at the Polls* (Philadelphia: Westminster Press, 1977).

Chapter 6
THE KENNEDY LEGACY

It is beyond the purview of this book to consider President Kennedy's place in the history of our nation. I leave that task to the historians of the future. But I am deeply disturbed by what appears to be a generalized downgrading or even repudiation of the legitimate achievements of a man still revered by millions of us for what he was and what he tried to accomplish.

In a recent article Henry Steele Commager reported the findings of the United States Historical Society's survey of our greatest presidents. "Most surprising" he says "was the comparatively low rating of the most glamorous of recent Presidents—the man who made Washington our Temporary Camelot—John F. Kennedy."[1] Commager adds insult to injury by omitting JFK from his list of "intellectual" presidents, though JFK read six books a week and won the Pulitzer Prize for Literature, an achievement shared by no other President.

The radical revisionists have just about succeded in destroying the image and record of JFK. Studies by John Berendt and Donald C. Lord established that anti-Kennedy bias has "been incorporated in the majority of textbooks used in American secondary and college classrooms."[2] This trend of the last decade seems to have reversed the initially favorable judgment given to Mr. Kennedy by the Organization of American Historians 1968 survey. At that time

Mr. Kennedy ranked first on flexibility, third on idealism, fifth on activeness, ninth on prestige, and tenth on strength of action. His overall ranking was ninth—in other words, one of the best U.S. presidents.[3]

Tom Wicker agrees with this assessment. "The idea that Kennedy was a minor figure of limited achievement is widely held today. ... Revisionism has taken most of the luster from the young President the nation mourned so deeply that long-ago November weekend."[4] Is this a fair assessment? An evaluation grounded in reality? I cannot agree.

John F. Kennedy should be remembered for the idealism, vigor, and intellectual acumen that he brought to his presidency. His emphasis on excellence, his ability to grow and change when new challenges required it, and his belief that each person can make a difference were attributes deserving of praise and appreciation.

Kennedy's willingness to jettison the uncreative anti-Communism of U.S. foreign policy and his recognition that civil rights was a moral crisis that demanded resolution should also assure him a place in history. Radical historians may berate him but there is hardly a black home in America without a pictorial memorial to the slain president. They knew, if today's revisionists do not, that they had a friend in the White House.

Furthermore, Kennedy's devotion to excellence can be seen in his appointments. Political scientist William G. Carleton wrote, "No administration in history staffed the executive departments and the White House offices with as many competent, dedicated and brilliant men as did Kennedy's. Kennedy paid little attention to party qualifications; the emphasis was on ability, drive, imagination, creativity."[5]

Kennedy cared deeply for the nation's reputation in cultural matters and its commitment to intellectual freedom—which he saw threatened by the Eisenhower-Nixon-McCarthy era. "Never before Kennedy's time has the White House paid so much personal and social attention to the nation's writers, artists, musicians, scientists, and scholars."[6] Richard Rovere says that Kennedy conceived of his role as an impresario of achievement in every area of American life, hoping that future presidents would continue this role.[7]

Kennedy was no dilettante, though. Carleton interprets JFK's mind as characterized by "rational and balanced thinking, objectivity, the ability to see all around a question, resilience, elusiveness, the capacity for keeping judgment in suspense, a detachment relating to one's self and one's own image, an avoidance of absolute commitment combined with genuine intellectual involvement, a general critical intelligence brought to bear on the findings of the specialists. ... He was a rationalist with a critical intelligence, a realist who knew the hard and subtle uses of power."[8]

Most interpreters of the Kennedy era have ignored what I believe to be his most enduring achievement. His election ratified and made credible America's image of itself as a nation predicated on religious tolerance and liberty. That image had been tarnished by restrictive political movements based on religious prejudice. The Kennedy election and the manner in which he sought to resolve long-standing interfaith and church-state disputes earn him a place in history.

His presidency substantially aided the development of pluralism. By breaking the unwritten law against non-Protestants, he severed the Protestant stranglehold on the White House and made it symbolically the genuine home of all Americans. He made it at least conceivable that members of other minority religious groups could aspire to the nation's highest elective office. He illuminated the discussion of church-state issues and brought them to the fore of public exposure. He proved that a Catholic president could be just as devoted to religious liberty as a non-Catholic, and his ecumenical posture furthered the cause of religious tolerance and understanding in America.

Did Kennedy's presidency *cause* or merely *coincide* with parallel movements within U.S. Catholicism? Was it a fluke of history or was it almost providential that JFK and Pope John were contemporaries? Historical judgments of this nature are difficult to make, but it is undeniable that JFK enhanced and gave impetus to the movements of interreligious harmony and Catholic liberalization. Cardinal Cushing subscribes to this view. "John F. Kennedy and Pope John XXIII were the great pioneers of what we now call the ecumenical spirit which is intended to wipe away all forms of

bigotry by knowing, respecting, and esteeming the religious beliefs of all peoples. ... I always felt that JFK was a forerunner in this field...because he never allowed his faith to interfere in any way with his relations with others. He was the greatest representative of brotherhood."[9]

Kennedy's record also had an indisputable and measurable impact on Catholic political attitudes. His adherence to relatively liberal goals and values gave them a new respectability in the Catholic community. Alfred O. Hero's *American Religious Groups View Foreign Policy*, (Duke University Press, 1973) charted the swing to the left among Catholics on international relations. The opinion change was most noticeable on the question of U.S. support for population control programs overseas.

Kennedy's impact on Catholicism should entitle him to a dramatic place in the annals of Catholic history. Andrew Greeley, in fact, suggests that Kennedy "spoke as a doctor of the Church, a teacher of the Church"[10] and adds, "In another age when the manner and purpose of canonization were different, John Kennedy would certainly be hailed as a saint."[11] Greeley admits that this apotheosis would cause JFK to roar with laughter.

In a somewhat more serious vein, though, I suggest that JFK should be regarded as a Catholic humanist statesman—as a man in the tradition of Thomas More, Lord Baltimore, Charles Carroll, and Lord Acton. That word "humanist" may frighten some contemporary readers whose experience of the word would imply a disbelief in a Supreme Being and a vigorous rejection of the supernatural, immortality of the soul, and a religion of revelation. As I use the term, I mean a concern and reverence for human values, an emphasis on the ethical in religion, and an orientation toward improving the human condition. In this sense Kennedy is no different from Erasmus or Jacques Maritain.

Kennedy's humanism was that of C. F. Potter, "faith in the supreme value and self-perfectibility of human personality."[12] Another attribute of humanism acceptable to JFK was its "confidence in human nature coupled with a belief in the power of education."[13] Donald C. Lord describes humanism as "an attitude which asserts that man is more important than abstract principles.

Throughout his public career John F. Kennedy was dedicated to this concept of humanism."[14]

What influence, if any, did JFK's religion have on his public policies or general political outlook? It is very difficult to assess this influence because Catholicism is capable of many political and social interpretations and one cannot say for sure that Kennedy is closer to the Catholic tradition than, say, Adenauer, DeGasperi, or DeGaulle. It is also impossible to say that Kennedy's position on civil rights, urban affairs, the Cuban quarantine, the Berlin Wall, the Nuclear Test Ban Treaty, or immigration reform was in any way altered or shaped by his religion. It is in fact quite unlikely. Public officials rarely make secular decisions with reference to personal religious sentiment. The general influence of religion on politics belongs to the realm of the subconscious, the imperceptible.

Kennedy's interpretation and adaptation of his Catholic heritage *did* play a role in the formation of his character. Dean Sayre's view comes close to mine. "I have come to a firm conclusion that [Kennedy's religion] was very profound. It was humanitarian in its first instinct, uninstructed technically, but yet very profound in his caring, in his concern. If one accepts a broad definition of Christianity and religion, I would say that President Kennedy was deeply religious in the most profound sense,...a man deeply rooted in moral principle, in good will, but not trained in the technicalities of theological subtlety."[15]

This view is reinforced by Brooks Hays's assessment, "No President ever tried harder to be President of all the people of all faiths than President Kennedy and no one...ever more faithfully interpreted our constitutional provisions with reference to church-state relations."[16]

A Catholic hero? Yes, and an American hero, too. It may be unfashionable at present to say that JFK was a great American and a good President but I have no hesitation in so affirming. In the words of Tom Wicker, "John Fitzgerald Kennedy was the last President the American people looked up to, in the old, unquestioning way. He was our young emperor, before the throne became bloodied and the cause tarnished by its own excesses. He was the last leader in a time when Americans were eager to follow."[17]

Notes

1. Henry Steele Commager, "Our Greatest Presidents," *Parade*, 8 May 1977.

2. Donald C. Lord, *John F. Kennedy* (Woodbury, NY: Barron, 1977); and, John Berendt, "A Look at the Record," *Esquire*, November 1973.

3. Barry M. Maranell, "The Evaluation of Presidents," *Journal of American History*, June 1970.

4. Tom Wicker, "Kennedy Without End, Amen," *Esquire*, June 1977.

5. William G. Carleton, "Kennedy in History," *The Antioch Review* 24 (Fall 1964): 286.

6. Ibid., p. 297.

7. Richard Rovere, "Letter from Washington," *The New Yorker*, 30 November 1963.

8. Carleton, "Kennedy in History," pp. 298-299.

9. Oral interview with Cardinal Cushing, Kennedy Library.

10. Andrew M. Greeley, *The Catholic Experience* (New York: Doubleday Image Books, 1969), p. 297.

11. Ibid., p. 280.

12. *Webster's New International Dictionary of the English Language*, 2d ed., s. v. humanism."

13. J. D. Douglas, ed., *The New International Dictionary of the Christian Church* (Grand Rapids, MI: Zondervan, 1974).

14. Lord, *John F. Kennedy*, p. 245.

15. Oral interview with Dean Francis Sayre, Kennedy Library.

16. Oral interview with Brooks Hays, Kennedy Library.

17. Wicker, "Kennedy Without End, Amen."

APPENDIX OF
PUBLIC ADDRESSES

From the more than one thousand public addresses and remarks delivered by President Kennedy, I have selected eight which relate to religion or religious issues in politics. Only one of these, the famous Houston address of September 12, 1960, has been reproduced several times. Those from the White House days were reprinted in the *Public Papers of the Presidents* series, published by the U.S. Government Printing Office; but they, too, have never been reprinted in a volume of this nature. The press conference following the Houston address was transcribed by the *New York Times* by telephone from the televised event in Houston and appeared in the September 14, 1960 issue. It has been edited slightly to make it more readable. It has never appeared in book form before. The April 21, 1960 address by Senator Kennedy to the American Society of Newspaper Editors on "The Religious Issue in American Politics" has likewise remained buried for over seventeen years. I discovered a copy in the Americans United archives, which was graciously given to the organization by the Senator's staff. It is one of the most significant of Mr. Kennedy's statements. The addresses have been chronologically arranged.

From the Office of Senator John F. Kennedy
Room 362, Senate Office Building
Washington, D. C.
FOR FLAT RELEASE AT 12:00 NOON (EST), THURSDAY,
APRIL 21, 1960

THE RELIGIOUS ISSUE IN AMERICAN POLITICS

[Following is the text of the address of Senator John F. Kennedy before the American Society of Newspaper Editors:]

I have decided, in view of current press reports, that it would be appropriate to speak with you today about what has widely been called "the religious issue" in American politics. The phrase covers a multitude of meanings. There is no religious *issue* in the sense that any of the major candidates differ on the role of religion in our political life. Every Presidential contender, I am certain, is dedicated to the separation of church and state, to the preservation of religious liberty, to an end to religious bigotry, and to the total independence of the office-holder from any form of ecclesiastical dictation.

Nor is there any real *issue* in the sense that any candidate is exploiting his religious affiliation. No one's candidacy, by itself, raises a religious issue. And I believe it is inaccurate to state that my "candidacy created the issue"—that, because I am replying to the bigots, I am now "running on the religious issue in West Virginia" —or that my statements in response to interrogation are "fanning the controversy." I am not "trying to be the first Catholic President," as some have written. I happen to believe I can serve my nation as President—and I also happen to have been born a Catholic.

Nor am I appealing, as is too often claimed, to a so-called Catholic vote. Even if such a vote exists—which I doubt—I want to make one thing clear again: I want no votes solely on account of my religion. Any voter, Catholic or otherwise, who feels another candidate would be a superior President should support that candidate. I do not want any vote cast for me for such a reason.

Neither do I want anyone to support my candidacy merely to prove that this nation is not bigoted—and that a Catholic can be elected President. I have never suggested that those opposed to me

are thereby anti-Catholic. There are ample legitimate grounds for supporting other candidates—(though I will not, of course, detail them here). Nor have I ever suggested that the Democratic Party is required to nominate me or face a Catholic revolt in November. I do not believe that to be true—I cannot believe our convention would act on such a premise—and I do believe that a majority of Americans of every faith will support the Democratic nominee, whoever he is.

What, then, is the so-called religious issue in American politics today? It is not, it seems to me, my actual religious convictions—but a misunderstanding of what those convictions actually are. It is not the actual existence of religious voting blocs—but a suspicion that such voting blocs may exist. And when we deal with such public fears and suspicions, the American press has a very grave responsibility.

I know the press did not create this religious issue. My religious affiliation is a fact—religious intolerance is a fact. And the proper role of the press is to report all facts that are a matter of public interest.

But the press has a responsibility, I think you will agree, which goes far beyond a reporting of the facts. It goes beyond lofty editorials deploring intolerance. For my religion is hardly, in this critical year of 1960, the dominant issue of our time. It is hardly the most important criterion—or even a relevant criterion—on which the American people should make their choice for Chief Executive. And the press, while not creating the issue, will largely determine whether or not it does become dominant—whether it is kept in perspective—whether it is considered objectively—whether needless fears and suspicions are stilled instead of aroused.

The members of the press should report the facts as they find them. They should describe the issues as they see them. But they should beware, it seems to me, of either magnifying this issue or oversimplifying it. They should beware of ignoring the vital issues of this campaign, while filling their pages with analyses that cannot be proven, with statements that cannot be documented and with an emphasis which cannot be justified.

I spoke in Wisconsin, for example, on farm legislation, foreign policy, defense, civil rights and several dozen other issues. The

people of Wisconsin seemed genuinely interested in these addresses. But I rarely found them reported in the press—except when they were occasionally sandwiched in between descriptions of my hand shaking, my theme-song, family haircut and, inevitably, my religion.

At almost every stop in Wisconsin I invited questions—and the questions came—on price supports, labor unions, disengagement, taxes and inflation. But these sessions were rarely reported in the press except when one topic was discussed: religion. An article, for example, supposedly summing the primary up in advance, mentioned the word Catholic twenty times in fifteen paragraphs—not mentioning even once dairy farms, disarmament, labor legislation or any other issue. And on the Sunday before the Primary, the Milwaukee Journal featured a map of the state, listing county by county the relating strength of three types of votes—Democrats, Republicans and Catholics.

In West Virginia, it is the same story. As reported in yesterday's *Washington Post*, the great bulk of West Virginians paid very little attention to my religion—until they read repeatedly in the nation's press that this was the decisive issue in West Virginia. There are many serious problems in that state—problems big enough to dominate any campaign—but religion is not one of them.

I do not think that religion is the decisive issue in any state. I do not think it should be. I do not think it should be made to be. And recognizing my own responsibilities in that regard, I am hopeful that you will recognize yours also.

For the past months and years, I have answered almost daily inquiries from the press about the religious issue. I want to take this opportunity to turn the tables—and to raise some questions for your thoughtful consideration.

First: Is the religious issue a legitimate issue in this campaign? There is only one legitimate question underlying all the rest: would you, as President of the United States, be responsive in any way to ecclesiastical pressures or obligations of any kind that might in any fashion influence or interfere with your conduct of that office in the national interest? I have answered that question many times. My answer was—and is—"NO."

Once that question is answered, there is no legitimate issue of my religion. But there are, I think, legitimate questions of public policy—of concern to religious groups which no one should feel bigoted about raising, and to which I do not object to answering. But I do object to being the only candidate required to answer those questions.

Federal assistance to parochial schools, for example, is a very legitimate issue actually before the Congress. I am opposed to it. I believe it is clearly unconstitutional. I voted against it on the Senate floor this year, when offered by Senator Morse. But interestingly enough, I was the *only* announced candidate in the Senate who did so. (Nevertheless I have not yet charged my opponents with taking orders from Rome.)

An Ambassador to the Vatican could conceivably become a real issue again. I am opposed to it, and said so long ago. But even though it was last proposed by a Baptist President, I know of no other candidate who has been even asked about this matter.

The prospects of any President ever receiving for his signature a bill providing foreign aid funds for birth control are very remote indeed. It is hardly the major issue some have suggested. Nevertheless I have made it clear that I would neither veto nor sign such a bill on any basis except what I considered to be the public interest, without regard to my private religious views. I have said the same about bills dealing with censorship, divorce, our relations with Spain or any other subject.

These are legitimate inquiries about real questions which the next President may conceivably have to face. But these inquiries ought to be directed equally to all candidates. I have made it clear that I strongly support—out of conviction as well as Constitutional obligation—the guarantees of religious equality provided by the First Amendment—and I ask only that these same guarantees be extended to me.

Secondly: Can we justify analyzing voters as well as candidates strictly in terms of their religion? I think the voters of Wisconsin objected to being categorized simply as either Catholics or Protestants in analyzing their political choices. I think they objected to being accosted by reporters outside of political meetings and asked

one question only—their religion—not their occupation or education or philosophy or income—only their religion.

And I think they had a right to object. The flood of post-primary analyses on the so-called "Catholic vote" and "Protestant vote" —carefully shaped to conform with their authors' pre-primary predictions—would never be published in any competent statistical journal.

Only this week, I received a very careful analysis of the Wisconsin results. It conclusively shows two significant patterns of bloc voting: I ran strongest in those areas where the average temperature in January was twenty degrees or higher, and poorest in those areas where it was fourteen degrees or lower—and that I ran well in the beech tree and basswood counties and not so well among the hemlock and pine.

Anyone who thinks these trends are merely coincidences of no relevance has never tried to campaign in Wisconsin in January. In any event, this analysis is being rushed to West Virginia, where I am assured that the winter is less severe and the basswood are abundant. It has been suggested, however, that to offset my apparent political handicaps I may have to pick a running mate from Maine or, preferably, Alaska.

The facts of the matter are that this analysis stands up statistically much better than all the so-called analyses of the religious vote. And so do analyses of each county based on their distance from the Minnesota border, the length of their Democratic tradition and their inclusion in my campaign itinerary. I carried some areas with large proportions of voters who are Catholics—and I lost some. I carried some areas where Protestants predominate—and I lost some.

It is true that I ran well in cities—and large numbers of Catholics live in cities. But so do union members and older voters and veterans and chess fans and basswood lovers. To say my support in the cities is due only to the religion of the voters is incapable of proof and an unfair indictment of their political maturity.

Of those Catholics who voted for me, how many did so on grounds of my religion—how many because they felt my opponent was too radical—how many because they resented the attacks on my record—how many because they were union members—how

many for some other reason? I do not know. And the facts are that *no one* knows.

For voters are more than Catholics, Protestants or Jews. They make up their minds for many diverse reasons, good and bad. To submit the candidates to a religious test is unfair enough—to apply it to the voters themselves is divisive, degrading and wholly unwarranted.

Third and finally: Is there any justification for applying special religious tests to one office only: the Presidency? Little or no attention was paid to my religion when I took the oath as Senator in 1953—as a Congressman in 1947—or as a Naval officer in 1941. Members of my faith abound in public office at every level except the White House. What is there about the Presidency that justifies this constant emphasis upon a candidate's religion and that of his supporters?

The Presidency is not, after all, the British Crown, serving a dual capacity in both church and state. The President is not elected to be protector of the faith—or guardian of the public morals. His attendance at church on Sunday should be his business alone, not a showcase for the nation.

On the other hand, we are in no danger of a one-man Constitutional upheaval. The President, however intent he may be on subverting our institutions, cannot ignore the Congress—or the voters—or the courts. And our highest court, incidentally, has a long history of Catholic Justices, none of whom, as far as I know, was ever challenged on the fairness of his Rulings on sensitive church-state issues.

Some may say we treat the Presidency differently because we have had only one previous Catholic candidate for President. But I am growing weary of that term. I am not the Catholic candidate for President. I do not speak for the Catholic Church on issues of public policy—and no one in that Church speaks for me. My record on aid to education, aid to Tito, the Conant nomination and other issues has displeased some prominent Catholic clergymen and organizations; and it has been approved by others. The fact is that the Catholic Church is not a monolith—it is committed in this country to the principles of individual liberty—and it has no claim over my conduct as a public officer sworn to do the public interest.

So I hope we can see the beginning of the end of references to me as "the Catholic candidate" for President. Do not expect me to explain or defend every act or statement of every Pope or priest, in this country or some other, in this century or the last—and that includes the Mayor of Dijon.

* * *

I have tried to examine with you today the press' responsibility in meeting this religious issue. The question remains: what is *my* responsibility? I am a candidate. The issue is here. Two alternatives have been suggested:

(1) The first suggestion is that I withdraw to avoid a "dangerous religious controversy"; and accept the Vice Presidential nomination in order to placate the so-called Catholic vote.

I find that suggestion highly distasteful. It assumes the worst about a country which prides itself on being more tolerant and better educated than it was in 1928. It assumes that Catholics are a pawn on the political chess-board, moved hither and yon, and somehow "bought off" by the party putting in the second-spot a Catholic whom the party barred from the top. And it forgets, finally, that such a performance would have an effect on our image abroad as well as our self-respect here at home.

Are we going to admit to the world that a Jew can be elected Mayor of Dublin, a Protestant can be chosen Foreign Minister of France, a Moslem can serve in the Israeli Parliament—but a Catholic cannot be President of the United States? Are we to tell Chancellor Adenauer, for example, that we want him risking his all on our front-lines; but that—if he were an American—we would never entrust him with our Presidency—nor would we accept our distinguished guest, Gen. DeGaulle? Are we to admit to the world—worse still, are we to admit to ourselves—that one-third of our population is forever barred from the White House?

So I am not impressed by those pleas that I settle for the Vice Presidency in order to avert a religious spectacle. Surely those who believe it dangerous to elect a Catholic as President will not want him to serve as Vice President, a heart-beat away from the office.

(2) The alternative is to proceed with the primaries, the convention and the election. If there is bigotry in the country, then so be it—there is bigotry. If that bigotry is too great to permit the fair

consideration of a Catholic who has made clear his complete independence and his complete dedication to separation of church and state, then we ought to know it.

But I do not believe that this is the case. I believe the American people are more concerned with a man's views and abilities than with the church to which he belongs. I believe that the founding fathers meant it when they provided in Article VI of the Constitution that there should be no religious test for public office—a provision that brought not one dissenting vote, only the comment of Roger Sherman that it was surely unnecessary in view of the liberality prevailing in each state. And I believe that the American people mean to adhere to those principles today.

But regardless of the political outcome, this issue is here to be faced. It is my job to face it frankly and fully. And it is your job to face it fairly, in perspective and in proportion.

I am confident that the press and other media of this country will recognize their responsibilities in this area—to refute falsehood, to inform the ignorant, and to concentrate on the issues, the *real* issues, in this hour of the nation's peril.

KENNEDY'S HOUSTON SPEECH

I am grateful for your generous invitation to state my views. While the so-called religious issue is necessarily and properly the chief topic here tonight, I want to emphasize from the outset that we have far more critical issues to face in the 1960 election: The spread of Communist influence, until it now festers ninety miles off the coast of Florida—the humiliating treatment of our president and vice president by those who no longer respect our power—the hungry children I saw in West Virginia, the old people who cannot pay their doctor bills, the families forced to give up their farms—an America with too many slums, with too few schools, and too late to the moon and outer space.

These are the real issues which should decide this campaign. And they are not religious issues—for war and hunger and ignorance and despair know no religious barriers.

But because I am a Catholic, and no Catholic has ever been elected president, the real issues in this campaign have been ob-

scured—perhaps deliberately, in some quarters less responsible than this. So it is apparently necessary for me to state once again—not what kind of church I believe in, for that should be important only to me—but what kind of America I believe in.

I believe in an America where the separation of church and state is absolute—where no Catholic prelate would tell the president (should he be Catholic) how to act, and no Protestant minister would tell his parishioners for whom to vote—where no church or church school is granted any public funds or political preference—and where no man is denied public office merely because his religion differs from the president who might appoint him or the people who might elect him.

I believe in an America that is officially neither Catholic, Protestant nor Jewish—where no public official either requests or accepts instructions on public policy from the pope, the National Council of Churches or any other ecclesiastical source—where no religious body seeks to impose its will directly or indirectly upon the general populace or the public acts of its officials—and where religious liberty is so indivisible that an act against one church is treated as an act against all.

For, while this year it may be a Catholic against whom the finger of suspicion is pointed, in other years it has been, and may someday be again, a Jew—or a Quaker—or a Unitarian—or a Baptist. It was Virginia's harassment of Baptist preachers, for example, that helped lead to Jefferson's Statute of Religious Freedom. Today I may be the victim—but tomorrow it may be you—until the whole fabric of our harmonious society is ripped at a time of great national peril.

Finally, I believe in an America where religious intolerance will someday end—where all men and all churches are treated as equals—where every man has the same right to attend or not attend the church of his choice—where there is no Catholic vote, no anti-Catholic vote, no bloc voting of any kind—and where Catholics, Protestants and Jews, at both the lay and pastoral level, will refrain from those attitudes of disdain and division which have no often marred their works in the past, and promote instead the American ideal of brotherhood.

That is the kind of America in which I believe, and it represents the kind of presidency in which I believe—a great office that must neither be humbled by making it the instrument of any one religious group, nor tarnished by arbitrarily withholding its occupancy from the members of any one religious group. I believe in a president whose religious views are his own private affair, neither imposed by him upon the nation nor imposed by the nation upon him as a condition to holding that office.

I would not look with favor upon a president working to subvert the First Amendment's guarantees of religious liberty. Nor would our system of checks and balances permit him to do so—and neither do I look with favor upon those who would work to subvert Article VI of the Constitution by requiring a religious test—even by indirection—for it. If they disagree with that safeguard, they should be out openly working to repeal it.

I want a chief executive whose public acts are responsible to all groups and obligated to none—who can attend any ceremony, service or dinner his office may appropriately require of him—and whose fulfillment of his presidential oath is not limited or conditioned by any religious oath, ritual or obligation.

This is the kind of America I believe in—and this is the kind I fought for in the South Pacific and the kind my brother died for in Europe. No one suggested then that we might have a "divided loyalty," that we did "not believe in liberty" or that we belonged to a disloyal group that threatened the "freedoms for which our forefathers died."

And in fact this is the kind of America for which our forefathers died—when they fled here to escape religious test oaths that denied office to members of less favored churches—when they fought for the Constitution, the Bill of Rights, and the Virginia Statute of Religious Freedom—and when they fought at the shrine I visited today, the Alamo. For side by side with Bowie and Crockett died McCafferty and Bailey and Carey—but no one knows whether they were Catholics or not. For there was no religious test at the Alamo.

I ask you tonight to follow in that tradition—to judge me on the basis of my record of fourteen years in Congress—on my declared stands against an ambassador to the Vatican, against unconstitu-

tional aid to parochial schools, and against any boycott of the public schools (which I have attended myself)—instead of judging me on the basis of these pamphlets and publications we all have seen that carefully select quotations out of context from the statements of Catholic church leaders, usually in other countries, frequently in other centuries and rarely relevant to any situation here—and always omitting, of course, the statement of the American Bishops in 1948 which strongly endorsed church-state separation, and which more nearly reflects the views of almost every American Catholic. I do not consider these other quotations binding upon my public acts—why should you? But let me say with respect to other countries, that I am wholly opposed to the state being used by any religious group, Catholic or Protestant, to compel, prohibit or persecute the free exercise of any other religion. And I hope that you and I condemn with equal fervor those nations which deny their presidency to Protestants and those which deny it to Catholics. And rather than cite the misdeeds of those who differ, I would cite the record of the Catholic Church in such nations as Ireland and France—and the independence of such statesmen as Adenauer and DeGaulle.

But let me stress again that these are my views—for, contrary to common newspaper usage, I am not the Catholic candidate for president. I am the Democratic party's candidate for president, who happens also to be a Catholic. I do not speak for my church on public matters—and the church does not speak for me.

Whatever issue may come before me as president—on birth control, divorce, censorship, gambling, or any other subject—I will make my decision in accordance with these views, in accordance with what my conscience tells me to be the national interest, and without regard to outside religious pressures or dictates. And no power or threat of punishment could cause me to decide otherwise.

But if the time should ever come—and I do not concede any conflict to be even remotely possible—when my office would require me to either violate my conscience or violate the national interest, then I would resign the office; and I hope any conscientious public servant would do the same.

But I do not intend to apologize for these views to my critics of either Catholic or Protestant faith—nor do I intend to disavow

either my views or my church in order to win this election. If I should lose on the real issues, I shall return to my seat in the Senate, satisfied that I had tried my best and was fairly judged. But if this election is decided on the basis that forty million Americans lost their chance of being president on the day they were baptized, then it is the whole nation that will be the loser, in the eyes of Catholics and non-Catholics around the world, in the eyes of history, and in the eyes of our own people.

But if, on the other hand, I should win the election, then I shall devote every effort of mind and spirit to fulfilling the oath of the presidency—practically identical, I might add, to the oath I have taken for fourteen years in the Congress. For, without reservation, I can "solemnly swear that I will faithfully execute the office of president of the United States, and will to the best of my ability preserve, protect and defend the Constitution...so help me God."

TRANSCRIPT OF TEXAS MINISTERS' QUERIES AT HOUSTON

Following is a transcription of Senator John F. Kennedy's replies to questions asked him Monday night by members of the Houston Ministerial Association at a meeting in the Rice Hotel, Houston, Tex. The questions and answers, televised in Texas, were recorded over a telephone line by The New York Times.

Q.—I think I speak for many that do not in any sense discount or in any sense doubt your loyalty and your love to this nation, or your position that's in accord with our position with regard to separation of church and state. But could I bring it down to where we stand right here tonight as two men of just nearly equal age just standing facing each other. If this meeting tonight were being held in the sanctuary of my church—it's the policy in my city that has many very fine Catholics in it—but the policy of the Catholic leadership forbids them to attend a Protestant service. If we tonight were in the sanctuary of my church right behind where we are, would you and could you attend as you have here?

SENATOR KENNEDY—Yes, I could. Now I can attend any— as I said in my statement I would attend any service that had any connection with my public office or in the case of a private cere-

mony, weddings, funerals, and so on, of course I would participate, and have participated. I think the only question would be whether I could participate as a participant—a believer—in your faith and maintain my membership in my church. That seems to me comes within the private beliefs that a Catholic might have. But as far as whether I could attend this sort of a function in your church, whether I as Senator or President could attend a function in your service connected with my position of office, then I could attend and would attend.

Q.—Very closely allied to it was the position with regard to the Chapel of the Chaplains [in Philadelphia] that was dedicated, which I believe you once accepted the invitation to attend—A.— That's right.

Q.—And then the press had said, I believe, Cardinal Dougherty brought pressure and you refused [the invitation] and did not attend?

A.—I'd be delighted to explain because that seems to be a matter of great interest.

I was invited in 1947, after my election to the Congress, by Dr. Daniel A. Poling to attend a dinner to raise funds for an interfaith chapel in honor of the four chaplains who went down on the Dorchester. That was fourteen years ago.

I was delighted to accept because I thought it was a useful and worthwhile cause. A few days before I was due to accept, I learned through my administrative assistant, who had friends in Philadelphia, two things:

first, that I was listed—and this is in Dr. Poling's book in which he describes the incident—as the spokesman for the Catholic faith at the dinner. Charles Taft, Senator Taft's brother, was to be the spokesman for the Protestant faith. Senator Lehman was to be the spokesman for the Jewish faith.

The second thing I learned was that the chapel, instead of being located as I thought it was as an interfaith chapel, was located in the basement of another church. It was not in that sense in a faith chapel, and for the fourteen years since that chapel was built there has never been a service of my church because of the physical location.

I therefore informed Dr. Poling that while I would be glad to come as a citizen—in fact many Catholics did go to the dinner—I

did not feel that I had very good credentials to attend as the spokesman for the Catholic faith at that dinner to raise funds when the whole Catholic church group in Philadelphia were not participating, and because the chapel has never been blessed or consecrated.

Now, I want to make it clear that my grounds for not going were private. I had no credentials to speak for the Catholic faith at a dinner for a chapel at which no Catholic service has ever been held, so that, until this day, unfortunately, no service has been held at the present time.

Q.—Mr. Kennedy, [Canon Rutenbahr of Christ Church Cathedral here in Houston.] I've read this platform and the planks in it with great interest, and especially in the realms of freedom. And I note that in the educational section, the right of education for each person is guaranteed or offered for a guarantee. It also says that there shall be equal opportunity for employment. In another section it says there shall be equal rights to housing and recreation. All of these speak, I think, in a wonderful sense, to the freedom which we want to keep here in America.

Yet, on the other hand, there is in another place in the platform, I read these words: "We will repeal the authorization for right-to-work laws."

Now, it seems to me that in this aspect here, and I feel that these are much more important than any religious issue, here you are abolishing an open shop. You are taking away the freedom of the individual worker, whether he wants to work and wants to belong to this union or not.

Now, isn't this sort of double talk? You're guaranteeing freedom on the one hand, and yet you're going to take it away on the other.

A.—No, I don't agree with that.

Q.—I think there's a dichotomy here in the platform.

A.—Well, that provision's been in the platform since 1948. And I'm sure there's a difference of opinion between us on that matter and between many Democrats on that matter.

But I think that it's a decision which goes to economic and political views. I don't think it involves a constitutional guarantee of freedom.

In other words, under the provisions of the Taft-Hartley Law a state was permitted to prohibit a union shop. But it was not permitted to guarantee a closed shop.

Now, my own judgment is that uniformity in interstate commerce is valuable. And therefore, I hold with the view that it's better to have uniform laws and not a law which is, in interstate commerce, and these are all—this is not intra, but it's interstate commerce—which permits one condition in one state and another in another.

This is not a new provision. It's been in for the last three platforms.

Q.—I am pastor of First Church of God here in Houston, and a member of the Houston Association of Ministers.

Mr. Kennedy, you very clearly stated your position tonight in regard to the propagation of the Gospel by all religious groups in other countries, and I appreciated that much because we Protestants are a missionary people.

However, the question I have to ask is this: if you are elected President, will you use your influence to get the Roman Catholic countries of South America and Spain to stop persecuting Protestant missionaries and to give equal rights to Protestants to propagate their faith as the United States gives to the Roman Catholic or any other group?

A.—I would use my influence as President of the United States to permit, to encourage the development of freedom all over the world. One of the rights which I consider to be important is the right of free speech, the right of assembly, the right of free religious practice, and I would hope that the United States and the President would stand for those rights all around the globe, without regard to geography or religion, or critical position.

Q.—Thank you.

Q.—Mr. Kennedy, this is V. H. Westmore, pastor of the Southmay Baptist Curch here in Houston, I have received today a copy of a resolution passed by the Baptist Pastors Conference of St. Louis and they are going to confront you with this tomorrow night. I would like for you to answer to the Houston crowd before you get to St. Louis.

This is the resolution: With deep sincerity and in Christian grace we plead with Senator John F. Kennedy, as the person presently concerned in this matter, to appeal to Cardinal Cushing, Mr. Kennedy's own hierarchical superior in Boston, to present to the

Vatican Mr. Kennedy's sincere statement relative to the separation of church and state in the United States and religious freedom as represented in the Constitution of the United States in order that the Vatican may officially authorize such a belief for all Roman Catholics in the United States.''

A.—May I just say, as I do not accept the right of, as I said, any ecclesiastical official to tell me what I shall do in the sphere of my public responsibility as an elected official, I do not propose also to ask Cardinal Cushing to ask the Vatican to take some action. I do not propose to interfere with their free right to do exactly what they want. There's no doubt in my mind that the viewpoint that I have expressed [applause] tonight publicly represents the opinion of the overwhelming majority of American Catholics, and I have no doubt my view is known to Catholics around the world. I'm just hopeful that by my stating it quite precisely—and I believe I stated it in the tradition of the American Catholics way back all the way to Bishop John Carroll—I feel that I hope this will clarify it without my having to take the rather circuitous route. This is the position I think of the American Catholic Church in the United States with which I am associated.

Q.—We appreciate your forthright statement. May I say we have great admiration for you, but until we know this is the position of your church, because there will be many Catholics who will be appointed if you are elected President, we would like to know that they too are free to make such statements as you have been so courageous to make [Applause].

A.—So let me say that anyone that I would appoint to any office as a Senator, or as a President, would, I hope, hold the same view of the necessity of their living up to, not only the letter of the Constitution, but the spirit.

If I may say so, I am a Catholic. I've stated my view very clearly. I don't find any difficulty in stating that view. In my judgment, it is the view of American Catholics from one end of the country to the other.

Why? Because as long as I can state it in a way that is, I hope, satisfactory to you, why do you possibly doubt that I represent a viewpoint which is hostile to the Catholic Church of the United States?

I believe I'm stating the viewpoint the Catholics in this country hold toward the happy relationship, which exists between church and state.

Q.—Let me ask you, sir, do you state it with the approval of the Vatican?

A.—I don't have to have approval in that sense. But my judgment is that Cardinal Cushing, who is a Cardinal from the diocese of which I'm a member, would approve of this statement, in the same way that he approved of the 1948 statement of the Bishops.

In my judgment, and I'm not a student of theology, I am stating what I believe to be the position of—my personal position, and also the position of the great majority.

Q.—Today, I had a telephone conversation with Dr. Poling and received this telegram from him. I'm sure you would like to clear this matter up. Let me read briefly from his telegram.

"The memorandum on religion as an election issue prepared by Senator Kennedy's associates has a section on the Poling incident.

"This section contains serious factual errors. I believe the Senator will wish to correct the errors, or that he will wish to withdraw that section.

"The original draft of the program on the interfaith dinner held in the Bellevue-Stratford Hotel on Dec. 15, 1947, identified Mr. Kennedy, then Congressman from Massachusetts, as Hon. John F. Kennedy, Congressman from Massachusetts. Mr. Kennedy was never invited as an official representative of a religious organization, nor, indeed, as the spokesman for the Catholic faith.

"No speaker on that occasion—Catholic, Jew, or Protestant—was identified by his faith. When, two days before the dinner occasion, Mr. Kennedy canceled his engagement, he expressed his regret and grief, but stated that since His Eminence the Cardinal requested him not to come, he, as a loyal son of the Church, had no other alternative.

"Therefore it was necessary to destroy this first program and to reprint."

A.—Now, I will state again the words that I used, or a quotation from the Rev. Poling's book, as spokesman for the Catholic faith. A book which was produced about a year ago, which first discussed this incident.

Secondly, my memory of the incident is quite clear. In fact, it's as good as Rev. Poling's. Because when the matter was first discussed, Rev. Poling stated that the incident took place in 1950. And it's only in the last two months that it has come forward that the incident took place in 1947.

Thirdly, I never discussed the matter with Cardinal Dougherty in my life. I've never spoken to the Cardinal. I first learned of it through Mr. Riordan who was my administrative assistant, who knew of Mr. Doyle, who worked for the National Catholic Welfare Conference, who stated that there was a good deal of concern among many of the church people in Philadelphia because of the location of the chapel, and because no service would ever be held in it because it was located in the basement of another church.

It was an entirely different situation than the one that I had confronted when I first happily accepted it.

Now there were three speakers—Kennedy was one of them, Taft was the second, Senator Lehman was the third. I don't think I've mistated that one of them was supposed to speak for the Catholic faith, as a spokesman, in Mr. Poling's words, one of them for the Protestant faith, and one for the Jewish faith.

Now, all I can say to you, sir, is for this chapel—I was glad to accept the invitation. I did not clear the invitation with anyone. It was only when I was informed that I was speaking, and I was invited, obviously, as a serviceman because I came from a prominent Catholic family, that I was informed that I was there really in a sense without any credentials.

The chapel, as I have said, has never had a Catholic service. It is not an interfaith chapel. And therefore for me to participate as a spokesman in that sense for the Catholic faith, I think would have given an erroneous impression.

Now, I've been there fourteen years. This took place in 1947 for I'd been in politics probably two months, and was relatively inexperienced. I should have inquired before getting into the incident. Is this the only incident that can be shown?" [Applause.]

This was a private dinner. This was not a public dinner. This was a private dinner which did not involve my responsibilities as a public official. My judgment was bad only in accepting it without having all the facts, which I wouldn't have done at a later date. But

I do want to say that I've been there for fourteen years. I have voted on hundreds of matters, probably thousands of matters, which involve all kinds of public questions, some of which border on the relationship between church and state, and quite obviously that record must be reasonably good or we wouldn't keep hearing about the Poling incident.

I don't mean to be disrespectful to Reverend Poling. I have high regard for his son. I have high regard for Dr. Poling. I don't like to be in a debate with him about it, but I must say, even looking back, I think it was imprudent of me to have accepted without more information, but I don't really feel that it demonstrates unfitness to hold a public office.

Q.—The reason for our concern is the fact that your church has stated that it has the privilege and the right and the responsibility to direct its members in various areas of life including the political realm. But we believe that history and observation indicate that it has done so, and we raise the question because we would like to know if you are elected President and your church elects to use that privilege and obligation, what your response will be under those circumstances.

A.—If my church attempted to influence me in a way which was improper or which affected adversely my responsibilities as a public servant sworn to uphold the Constitution, then I would reply to them that this was an improper action on their part. It was one to which I could not subscribe, that I was opposed to it, and that it would be an unfortunate breach of—an interference with—the American political system.

I'm confident that there would be no such interference.

We've had two Chief Justices of the Supreme Court who were Catholics. We've had three Prime Ministers of Canada in this century. I've already mentioned Mr. de Gaulle and Mr. Adenauer. My judgment is that an American who is a Catholic, who is as sensitive as a Catholic must be who seeks this high office, as exposed to the pressures which whirl around us, he will be extremely diligent in his protection of the Constitutional separation.

Q.—We would be most happy to have such a statement from the Vatican.

Q.—Because of the briefness of the time, let's cut out the applause.

Q.—Senator Kennedy, V. E. Howard, minister of the Church of Christ. First of all I should like to quote some authoritative quotations from Catholic sources, and then propose the question.

"So that a false statement knowingly made to one who has not a right to the truth will not be a lie"—*Catholic Encyclopedia*, vol. 10, page 696. Quoting: "However, we are also under an obligation to keep secrets faithfully and sometimes the easiest way of fulfilling that duty is to say what is false or tell a lie." *Catholic Encyclopedia*, Vol. 10, page 195. "When mental reservation is permissible it is lawful to cooperate one's utterances by an oath if there be an adequate cause."—Article on perjury, *Catholic Encyclopedia* Vol. 11, page 696. Quoting again, "The truth we proclaim under oath is relative and not absolute."—Explanation of Catholic Morals, page 130.

Just recently from the Vatican in Rome this news release was given from the official Vatican newspaper, and I am quoting that of date May 19, 1960, Tuesday, that the Roman Catholic hierarchy had the right and duty to intervene in the political field to guide its flock. The newspaper rejected what is termed "the absurd split of conscience between the believer and the citizen."

However, *Osservatore Romano* made it clear that its announcement was valid for Roman Catholic laymen everywhere. It deplored the great confusion of ideas that is spreading especially between Catholic doctrine and social and political activities and between the ecclesiastical hierarchy and the lay faithful in the civil field.

Pope John XXIII recently gave this statement, I quote you *The St. Louis Review*, date of Dec. 12, 1958, "Catholics may unite their strength toward the common aid and the Catholic hierarchy has the right and duty of guiding them." Question, sir: Do you subscribe to the doctrine of mental reservation which I have quoted from the Catholic authorities? Do you submit to the authority of the present Pope which I have quoted from in these quotations?

A.—Well, let me say in the first place I've not read *The Catholic Encyclopedia* and I don't know all the quotations which you're giving me. I don't agree with the statement. I find no difficulty in saying so. But I do think probably I can get a, make a, better comment if I had the entire quotation before me. But in any case, I had not read it before and if the quotation is meant to imply that

when you take an oath you don't mean it or that it's proper for you to take oaths and then break them, it's proper for you to lie, if that is what this states—and I don't know whether that's what it states unless I read it all in context—and then of course I would not agree with it.

Secondly, on the question of the *Osservatore Romano* article, once again I don't have that in full.

I read the statement of last December which was directed to a situation in Sicily where some of the Catholics were active in the Communist party. But I'm not familiar with the one of May, 1960, that you mention. In any case the *Osservatore Romano* has no standing as far as binding me.

Thirdly, quotation of Pope John of 1958—I didn't catch all of that. If you'll read that again, I'll tell you whether I support that or not.

Q.—Pope John XXIII only recently stated, according to *St. Louis Review* dated Dec. 12, 1958: "Catholics must unite their strength toward the common aim and the Catholic hierarchy has the right and duty of guiding them." Do you subscribe to that?

A.—Well, now, I don't, I couldn't describe guiding them in what area. If you're talking about in the area of faith and morals, in the instructions of the church, I would think any Baptist minister or Congregational minister has the right and duty to try to guide his flock. If you mean by that statement that the Pope or anyone else could bind me by a statement, in the fulfillment of my public duties, I say, "no."

If that statement is intended to mean, and it's very difficult to comment on a sentence taken out of an article which I have not read, but if that is intended to imply that the hierarchy has some obligations, or has an obligation, to attempt to guide the members of the Catholic Church, then that may be proper.

But it all depends on the previous language of what you mean by "guide." If you mean direct, or instruct, on matters dealing with the organization of the faith, the details of the faith, then, of course, they have that obligation. If you mean that anyone could guide or direct me in fulfilling my public duty, then I do not agree.

Q.—Thank you, sir. Then you do not agree with the Pope on that statement.

A.—Gentlemen, now that's why I wanted to be careful because that statement, it seems to me, is taken out of the context that you just made to me. I could not tell you what the Pope meant unless I had the entire article. I would be glad to state to you that no one can direct me in the fulfillment of my duties, as a public official under the United States Constitution, that I am directed to do to the people of the United States, sworn to by an oath to God. Now that is my flat statement. I would not want to go into details on a sentence that you read to me which I may not understand completely.

Q.—We have time for one more question if it can be handled briefly.

Q.—Senator Kennedy: Robert McClaren from Westminster Presbyterian Church here in Houston.

You have been quite clear and I think laudably so on this matter of the separation of church and state, and you have answered very graciously the many questions that have come up around it. There is one question, however, which seems to me quite relevant and this relates to your statement that if you found by some remote possibility a real conflict between your oath of office as President that you would resign that office, if it were in real conflict with your church.

A.—No, I said with my conscience.

Q.—With your conscience?

A.—Yes.

Q.—In the syllabus of errors of Pope Leo IX which *The Catholic Encyclopedia* states is still binding, (although it is from a different century, it is still binding upon all Catholics) there are three very specific things which are denounced, including the separation of state and church, the freedom of religions other than Catholicism to propagate themselves, and the freedom of conscience. Do you still feel these binding upon you, that you hold your oath of office above your allegiance to the Pope on these issues?

A.—Well, let's go through the issues, because I don't think there's a conflict on these three issues. The first issue, as I understand it was on the relationship between the Catholic and the state and other faiths, was that it?

Q.—No, the separation of church and state.

A.—I support that, and in my judgment the American Bishops' statement of 1948 clearly supported it. That in my judgment is the view held by Catholics in this country. They support the Constitution on separation of church and state and they are not in error in that regard.

Q.—The second was the right of religions other than Roman Catholic to propagate themselves.

A.—I think they should be permitted to propagate themselves, any faith, without any limitations by the power of the state or encouragement by the power of the state. What was the third?

Q.—The third was the freedom of conscience in matters of religion and this also in Point 46, I believe it is, extends to freedom of the mind in the realms of science.

A.—Yes, well I believe in freedom of conscience. Let me just, I guess our time is coming to an end, but I believe in it. Let me state finally that I am delighted to come here today. I don't want anyone to think because they interrogate me on this very important question that I regard that as unfair questions, or unreasonable, or that if somebody who is concerned about the matter is prejudiced or bigoted. I think this fight for religious freedom is basic in the establishment of the American system, and therefore any candidate for the office, I think, should submit himself to the questions of any reasonable man. My only objection would be...[applause].

My only limit to that would be that, if somebody said, "Regardless of Senator Kennedy's position, regardless of how much evidence he's given that if what he says he means, I still wouldn't vote for him because he's a member of that church." I would consider that unreasonable.

What I consider to be reasonable and an exercise of free will and free choice is to ask the candidate to state his views as broadly as possible, investigate his record to see whether he states what he believes and then make an independent, rational judgment as to whether he could be entrusted with this highly important position.

So I want you to know that I am grateful to you for inviting me tonight. I'm sure that I have made no converts to my church, but I do hope that at least my view, is that which I believe to be the view of my fellow Catholics who hold office. I hope that it may be of some value in at least assisting you to make a careful judgment. Thank you.

REMARKS OF PRESIDENT JFK TO REPRESENTATIVES OF THE BAPTIST WORLD ALLIANCE AT THE WHITE HOUSE FEBRUARY 2, 1961

1. I welcome you here today not only because you represent a great cause but also because your being here is symbolic of a bond between your own work and mine—the mutual desire of each of us to share with the world those blessings, material and spiritual, that freedom has bestowed upon us.

2. Political freedom as we know it in America has always imposed upon us a grand imperative to help others to find their way to equal liberty. The Greeks said, "Those who have the torch must pass the light." This is no less true with the religious freedom we share, and I am proud that men and women like yourselves, born to freedom, have responded to an inner compulsion to share your faith and your freedom with others around the world.

3. Baptists in Colonial America contributed greatly to the concept of religious freedom that became an archstone of this Republic. Throughout our nation's history, your zealous missionary spirit has helped to lift our country's horizons to the larger responsibility we hold.

4. But this is no time to linger in the past. These are troubled days and men of freedom dare not try to live by bread alone. We need the courage and the compassion that spring from faith in the Creator. We need the sense of commitment, the feeling of urgency, the spirit of selflessness that have compelled each of you into missionary service.

5. As you return to your fields of labor, I hope you will be more than representatives of a single religious faith. For you serve under the burden of a dual responsibility—your obligations are not only to God but to your country as well. In revealing the best that is in your faith, you can also testify to the best that is in your country. You can witness to an Almighty God whose eyes behold no race, creed, or color; you can witness, too, to a Nation whose people have committed themselves to the defense and extension of human rights wherever men live in tyranny, wherever men long to be free.

REMARKS AT THE 11th ANNUAL PRESIDENTIAL
PRAYER BREAKFAST[1]
FEBRUARY 7, 1963

Senator Carlson, Mr. Vice President, Reverend Billy Graham, Mr.
Speaker, Mr. Chief Justice, gentlemen:

I am honored to be with you here again this morning. These
breakfasts are dedicated to prayer and all of us believe in and need
prayer. Of all the thousands of letters that are received in the office
of the President of the United States, letters of good will and
wishes, none, I am sure, have moved any of the incumbents half so
much as those that write that those of us who work here in behalf
of the country are remembered in their prayers.

You and I are charged with obligations to serve the Great Republic in years of great crisis. The problems we face are complex; the
pressures are immense, and both the perils and the opportunities
are greater than any nation ever faced. In such a time, the limits of
mere human endeavor become more apparent than ever. We
cannot depend solely on our material wealth, on our military
might, or on our intellectual skill or physical courage to see us
safely through the seas that we must sail in the months and years to
come.

Along with all of these we need faith. We need the faith with
which our first settlers crossed the sea to carve out a state in the
wilderness, a mission they said in the Pilgrims' Compact, the
Mayflower Compact, undertaken for the glory of God. We need
the faith with which our Founding Fathers proudly proclaimed the
independence of this country to what seemed at that time an almost
hopeless struggle, pledging their lives, their fortunes, and their

[1]The prayer breakfast of International Christian Leadership, Inc., a
nondenominational group of laymen, was held at the Mayflower Hotel in
Washington. In his opening words the President referred to Frank Carlson, U.S. Senator from Kansas, who served as chairman of the breakfast;
Vice President Lyndon B. Johnson; the Rev. William F. Graham, evangelist; John W. McCormack, Speaker of the House of Representatives; and
Earl Warren, Chief Justice of the United States. Later, in his remarks to
the ladies, he referred to Dr. Abraham Vereide, Secretary General of the
International Council for Christian Leaders.

sacred honor with a firm reliance on the protection of divine providence. We need the faith which has sustained and guided this Nation for 175 long and short years. We are all builders of the future, and whether we build as public servants or private citizens, whether we build at the national or the local level, whether we build in foreign or domestic affairs, we know the truth of the ancient Psalm, "Except the Lord build the house, they labour in vain that build it."

This morning we pray together; this evening apart. But each morning and each evening, let us remember the advice of my fellow Bostonian, the Reverend Phillips Brooks: "Do not pray for easy lives. Pray to be stronger men! Do not pray for tasks equal to your powers. Pray for powers equal to your tasks."

[The President spoke first to the gentlemen in the hotel's main ballroom and then to the ladies in the east room.]
Ladies:

I'm glad to be with you again this morning with the Vice President, Reverend Billy Graham, Dr. Vereide, Senator Carlson, the same quartet that was here last year and the year before.

I think these breakfasts serve a most useful cause in uniting us all on an occasion when we look not to ourselves but to above for assistance. On our way from the last meeting to this, we met two members of Parliament who carried with them a message from Lord Home to this breakfast, in which Lord Home quoted the Bible and said that perhaps the wisest thing that was said in the Bible was the words, "Peace, be still."

I think it's appropriate that we should on occasion be still and consider where we are, where we've been, what we believe in, what we are trying to work for, what we want for our country, what we want our country to be, what our individual responsibilities are, and what our national responsibilities are. This country has carried great responsibilities, particularly in the years since the end of the Second War, and I think that willingness to assume those responsibilities has come in part from the strong religious conviction which must carry with it a sense of responsibility to others if it is genuine, which has marked our country from its earliest beginnings, when the recognition of our obligation to God was stated in nearly every public document, down to the present day.

This is not an occasion for feeling pleased with ourselves, but, rather, it is an occasion for asking for help to continue our work and to do more. This is a country which has this feeling strongly. I mentioned in the other room the letters which I receive, which the Members of Congress receive, which the Governors receive, which carry with them by the hundreds the strong commitment to the good life and also the strong feeling of communication which so many of our citizens have with God, and the feeling that we are under His protection. This is, I think, a sourse of strength to us all.

I want to commend all that you do, not merely for gathering together this morning, but for all the work and works that make up part of your Christian commitment. I am very proud to be with you.

ADDRESS AT THE BOSTON COLLEGE CENTENNIAL CEREMONIES.[1] APRIL 20, 1963

Father Walsh, Your Eminence, Governor Peabody, members of the faculty, ladies and gentlemen—

It is a great pleasure to come back to a city where my accent is considered normal, and where they pronounce the words the way they are spelled!

I take especial satisfaction in this day. As the recipient of an honorary degree in 1956 from Boston College, and therefore an instant alumnus, I am particularly pleased to be with all of you on this most felicitous occasion.

---

[1]The President spoke at 2:45 p.m. in Alumni Stadium on the college campus at Newton, Massachusetts. His opening words referred to the Reverend Michael P. Walsh, S.J., President of Boston College; His Eminence Richard Cardinal Cushing, Archbishop of Boston; and Governor Endicott Peabody of Massachusetts. Later he referred to Nathan N. Pusey, President of Harvard University; the Very Reverend Edward B. Bunn, S.J., President of Georgetown University; and Lady Barbara Ward Jackson, noted British writer—all of whom were awarded honorary degrees by Boston College.

This university, or college, as Father Walsh has described, was founded in the darkest days of the Civil War, when this Nation was engaged in a climactic struggle to determine whether it would be half slave and half free or all free. And now, one hundred years later, after the most intense century perhaps in human history, we are faced with the great question of whether this world will be half slave and half free, or whether it will be all one or the other. And on this occasion, as in 1863, the services of Boston College are still greatly needed.

It is good also to participate in this ceremony which has honored three distinguished citizens of the free world—President Pusey, Father Bunn, and our friend from the world of freedom, Lady Jackson.

Boston College is a hundred years old—old by the life span of men, but young by that of universities. In this week of observance, you have rightly celebrated the achievements of the past, and equally rightly you have turned in a series of discussions by outstanding scholars to the problems of the present and the future. Learned men have been talking here of the knowledge explosion, and in all that they have said I am sure they have implied the heavy present responsibility of institutions like this one. Yet today I want to say a word on the same theme, to impress upon you as urgently as I can the growing and insistent importance of universities in our national life.

I speak of universities because that is what Boston College has long since become. But most of what I say applies to liberal arts colleges as well. My theme is not limited to any one class of universities, public or private, religious or secular. Our national tradition of variety in higher education shows no sign of weakening, and it remains the task of each of our institutions to shape its own role among its differing sisters.

In this hope I am much encouraged by a reading in this last week of the remarkable encyclical, "Pacem in Terris." In its penetrating analysis of today's great problems, of social welfare and human rights, of disarmament and international order and peace, that document surely shows that on the basis of one great faith and its traditions there can be developed counsel on public affairs that is of value to all men and women of good will. As a Catholic I am proud

of it; and as an American I have learned from it. It only adds to the impact of this message that it closely matches notable expressions of conviction and aspiration from churchmen of other faiths, as in recent documents of the World Council of Churches, and from outstanding world citizens with no ecclesiastical standing. We are learning to talk the language of progress and peace across the barriers of sect and creed. It seems reasonable to hope that a similar process may be taking place across the quite different barriers of higher learning.

From the office that I hold, in any case, there can be no doubt today of the growing meaning of universities in America. That, of course, is one basic reason for the increasing urgency with which those who care most for the progress of our society are pressing for more adequate programs in higher education and in education generally. It is for this reason that I urge upon everyone here and in this country the pressing need for national attention and a national decision in the national interest upon the national question of education. In at least four ways, the new realities of our day have combined to intensify the focal role of the university in our Nation's life.

First, and perhaps most obvious, the whole world has come to our doorstep and the universities must be its student. In the strange geometry of modern politics, the distant Congo can be as close to us as Canada, and Canada, itself, is worth more attention than we have sometimes given. Cultures not our own press for understanding. Crises we did not create require our participation. Accelerating change is the one universal human prospect. The universities must help.

Second, there is indeed an explosion of knowledge and its outward limits are not yet in sight. In some fields, progress seems very fast; in others, distressingly slow. It is no tribute to modern science to jump lightly to the conclusion that all its secrets of particle physics, of molecular life, of heredity, of outer space, are now within easy reach. The truth is more massive and less magical. It is that wherever we turn, in defense, in space, in medicine, in industry, in agriculture, and most of all in basic science, itself, the requirement is for better work, deeper understanding, higher education. And while I have framed this comment in the terms of the natural sciences, I insist, as do all those who live in this field, that at

every level of learning there must be an equal concern for history, for letters and the arts, and for man as a social being in the widest meaning of Aristotle's phrase. This also is the work of the university.

And third, as the world presses in and knowledge presses out, the role of the interpreter grows. Men can no longer know everything themselves; the 20th century has no universal man. All men today must learn to know through one another—to judge across their own ignorance—to comprehend at second hand. These arts are not easily learned. Those who would practice them must develop intensity of perception, variety of mental activity, and the habit of open concern for truth in all its forms. Where can we expect to find a training ground for this modern maturity, if not in our universities?

Fourth and finally, these new requirements strengthen still further what has always been a fundamental element in the life of American colleges and universities—that they should be dedicated to "the Nation's service." The phrase is Woodrow Wilson's, and no one has discussed its meaning better. What he said in 1896 is more relevant today than ever before, and I close with a quotation from him.

I offer it to you with renewed congratulations, and in the confident hope that as the second century opens, Boston College will continue to respond—as she did in her beginnings—to the new needs of the age.

"It is not learning," said President Wilson, "but the spirit of service that will give a college place in the public annals of the Nation." "It is indispensable," he said, "if it is to do its right service, that the air of affairs should be admitted to all its classrooms...the air of the world's transactions, the consciousness of the solidarity of the race, the sense of the duty of man toward man ...the promise and the hope that shine in the face of all knowledge. ... The days of glad expansion are gone, our life grows tense and difficult; our resource for the future lies in careful thought, providence, and a wise economy; and the school must be of the Nation."

Boston College for one hundred years has been of the Nation and so it will be for the next hundred.

Thank you.

STATEMENT BY THE PRESIDENT ON THE DEATH OF POPE JOHN XXIII.
JUNE 3, 1963

The highest work of any man is to protect and carry on the deepest spiritual heritage of the race. To Pope John was given the almost unique gift of enriching and enlarging that tradition. Armed with the humility and calm which surrounded his earliest days, he brought compassion and an understanding drawn from wide experience to the most devisive problems of a tumultuous age. He was the chosen leader of world Catholicism, but his concern for the human spirit transcended all boundaries of belief or geography. The ennobling precepts of his encyclicals and his actions drew on the accumulated wisdom of an ancient faith for guidance in the most complex and troublesome problems of the modern age. To him the divine spark which unites men would ultimately prove more enduring than the forces which divide. His wisdom, compassion, and kindly strength have bequeathed humanity a new legacy of purpose and courage for the future.

REMARKS IN NEW YORK CITY AT THE NATIONAL CONVENTION OF THE CATHOLIC YOUTH ORGANIZATION.[1]
NOVEMBER 15, 1963

Monsignor, Fathers, Sisters, fellow members of the CYO:

I am glad to be here today. I said to the Monsignor coming up that I was pleased to see the Sisters, that in my experience Monsignors and Bishops are all Republicans while Sisters are all Democrats! In any case I am glad to see you and I want to congratulate you on the effort that you are making.

The theme of this meeting is Youth gives Service, And I can't imagine a greater cause in which to be engaged, to give the best that

[1]The President spoke at 11:40 a.m. in the grand ballroom of the New York Hilton Hotel to the delegates to the 7th National CYO Convention. His opening word "Monsignor" refers to the Right Reverend Frederick J. Stevenson, National Director of the CYO.

you have, than for the United States. Because upon the United States rests not only the burdens of caring for 190 million people but also for hundreds of millions of people around the globe who today without hope look to the United States. Whatever we are able to do in this country, whatever success we are able to make of ourselves, whatever leadership we are able to give, whatever demonstration we can make that a free society can function and move ahead and provide a better life for its people—all those things that we do here have their effect all around the globe.

The world is engaged in the most difficult and trying struggle in its long history. All of the great epics which have torn the world for the last two thousand years pale in comparison to the great ideological gulf which separates us from those who oppose us. It is our responsibility not merely to denounce our enemies and those who make themselves our enemies but to make this system work, to demonstrate what freedom can do, what those who are committed to freedom and the future can do. So I realize that this meeting is not only a meeting of the youth today but those of whom we expect so much in the future.

Winston Churchill once said that democracy is the worst form of government except for all the other systems that have been tried. It is the most difficult. It requires more of you—discipline, character, self-restraint, a willingness to serve the public interest as well as our own private interests. All of these Priests and Sisters who have gathered you together from all over the United States don't do it merely because—even though they want you to do well—they don't do it merely because they want four or five thousand boys and girls to do well. It is because they regard you as the future leaders of the United States; as the future leaders of a great free country. That is why I come here today. Not just because you are doing well and because you are outstanding students, but because we expect something of you. And unless in this free country of ours we are able to demonstrate that we are able to make this society work and progress, unless we can hope that from you we are going to get back all of the talents which society has helped develop in you, then, quite obviously, all the hopes of all of us that freedom will not only endure but prevail, of course, will be disappointed.

So we ask the best of you. I hope you will spend your time now well, but I hope that in a long life that you will recognize your obligations to the Great Republic and to help those who need help, to help those millions of boys and girls who drop out of school, who can't find work, who live in underprivileged areas.

I have been impressed by the fact that we have been able to get ten thousand young men and women to go around the world as part of the Peace Corps. But look at all the sections of the United States, in our large cities, in eastern Kentucky, parts of southern Illinois, parts of Ohio, West Virginia, where people live lives of desperation without hope; they look to this country, they look to you, and they look to me to *serve*. So I hope that all of you will serve—serve not only your families, and your church, but also serve this country. It deserves the best. It has been very generous to us all. And we must be generous in return. So I congratulate you on what you have done, and most of all I congratulate you on what you are going to do.

Thank you.